Contents

Throughout the Articles references to footnotes brackets.

ARTICLES OF AGREEMENT		*Page* 5
Recitals (First – Seventh)		6
Articles		7
1	Contractor's obligations	
2	Contract Sum	
3	Architect	
4	Quantity Surveyor	
5	Dispute or difference – adjudication	
6·1	Planning Supervisor	
6·2	Principal Contractor	
7A	Dispute or difference – arbitration	
7B	Dispute or difference – legal proceedings	
Attestation		11

CONDITIONS: PART 1: GENERAL

1	**Interpretation, definitions etc.**	13
1·1	Method of reference to clauses	
1·2	Articles etc. to be read as a whole	
1·3	Definitions	
1·4	[Number not used]	
1·5	Contractor's responsibility	
1·6	Reappointment of Planning Supervisor or Principal Contractor – notification to Contractor	
1·7	Giving or service of notices or other documents	
1·8	Reckoning periods of days	
1·9	Employer's Representative	
1·10	Applicable law	
1·11	Electronic data interchange	
1·12	Contracts (Rights of Third Parties) Act 1999 – contracting out	
2	**Contractor's obligations**	17
2·1	Contract Documents	
2·2	·1 Contract Bills	
	·2 Preparation of Contract Bills	
2·3/2·4	Discrepancies in or divergences between documents	
3	**Contract Sum – additions or deductions – adjustment – Interim Certificates**	18
4	**Architect's instructions**	18
4·1	Compliance with Architect's instructions	
4·2	Provisions empowering instructions	
4·3	·1 Instructions to be in writing	
	·2 Procedure if instructions given otherwise than in writing	
5	**Contract Documents – other documents – issue of certificates**	19
5·1	Custody of Contract Bills and Contract Drawings	
5·2	Copies of documents	
5·3	Descriptive schedules etc. – master programme of Contractor	
5·4	·1 Information Release Schedule	
	·2 Provision of further drawings or details	
5·5	Availability of certain documents	
5·6	Return of drawings etc.	
5·7	Limits to use of documents	
5·8	Issue of Architect's certificates	
5·9	Supply of as-built drawings etc. – Performance Specified Work	
6	**Statutory obligations, notices, fees and charges**	20
6·1	·1/·5 Statutory Requirements	
	·6 Divergence – Statutory Requirements and the Contractor's Statement	
	·7 Change in Statutory Requirements after Base Date	
6·2	Fees or charges	
6·3	Exclusion of provisions on Domestic Sub-Contractors and Nominated Sub-Contractors	
6A	**Provisions for us that all the CDM Regulations apply**	
6A·1	Employer's obligation – Planning Supervisor – Principal Contractor	
6A·2	Contractor – compliance with duties of a principal contractor	
6A·3	Successor appointed to the Contractor as Principal Contractor	
6A·4	Health and safety file	
7	**Levels and setting out of the Works**	22
8	**Work, materials and goods**	22
8·1	·1/·3 Kinds and standards etc.	
	·4 Construction Skills Certification Scheme	
	·5 Substitution of materials or goods – Performance Specified Work	
8·2	·1 Vouchers – materials and goods	
	·2 Executed work	
8·3	Inspection – tests	
8·4	Powers of Architect – work not in accordance with the Contract	
8·5	Powers of Architect – non-compliance with clause 8·1·3	
8·6	Exclusion from the Works of persons employed thereon	
9	**Royalties and patent rights**	23
9·1	Treatment of royalties etc. – indemnity to Employer	
9·2	Architect's instructions – treatment of royalties etc.	
10	**Person-in-charge**	24
11	**Access for Architect to the Works**	24
12	**Clerk of works**	24
13	**Variations and provisional sums**	24
13·1	Definition of Variation	
13·2	Instructions requiring a Variation	
13·3	Instructions on provisional sums	
13·4	Valuation of Variations and provisional sum work and work covered by an Approximate Quantity	
13·5	Valuation rules	
13·6	Contractor's right to be present at measurement	
13·7	Valuations – Employer/Contractor agreement – 13A Quotation for a Variation and Variations thereto – addition to or deduction from Contract Sum	
13A	**Variation instruction – Contractor's quotation in compliance with the instruction**	29
13A·1	Contractor to submit his quotation ('13A Quotation')	
13A·2	Content of the Contractor's 13A Quotation	
13A·3	Acceptance of 13A Quotation – Architect's confirmed acceptance	
13A·4	Contractor's 13A Quotation not accepted	
13A·5	Payment for a 13A Quotation	
13A·6	Restriction on use of a 13A Quotation	
13A·7	Number of days – clauses 13A·1·1 and/or 13A·1·2	
13A·8	Variations to work for which a confirmed acceptance of a 13A Quotation has been issued – valuation	
14	**Contract Sum**	31
14·1	Quality and quantity of work included in Contract Sum	
14·2	Contract Sum – only adjusted under the Conditions – errors in computation	
15	**Value added tax – supplemental provisions**	31
15·1	Definitions – VAT Agreement	
15·2	Contract Sum – exclusive of VAT	

15·3	Possible exemption from VAT		
16	**Materials and goods unfixed or off-site**		*32*
16·1	Unfixed materials and goods – on site		
16·2	Unfixed materials and goods – off-site		
17	**Practical Completion and defects liability**		*32*
17·1	Certificate of Practical Completion		
17·2	Defects, shrinkages or other faults		
17·3	Defects etc. – Architect's instructions		
17·4	Certificate of Completion of Making Good Defects		
17·5	Damage by frost		
18	**Partial possession by Employer**		*33*
18·1	Employer's wish – Contractor's consent		
·1	Practical Completion – relevant part		
·2	Defects etc. – relevant part		
·3	Insurance – relevant part		
·4	Liquidated damages – relevant part		
19	**Assignment and sub-contracts**		*33*
19·1	Assignment		
19·2	Sub-letting – Domestic Sub-Contractors – Architect's consent		
19·3	Sub-letting – list in Contract Bills		
19·4	Sub-letting – conditions of any sub-letting		
19·5	Nominated Sub-Contractors		
20	**Injury to persons and property and indemnity to Employer**		*35*
20·1	Liability of Contractor – personal injury or death – indemnity to Employer		
20·2	Liability of Contractor – injury or damage to property – indemnity to Employer		
20·3	Injury or damage to property – exclusion of the Works and Site Materials		
21	**Insurance against injury to persons or property**		*36*
21·1	Contractor's insurance – personal injury or death – injury or damage to property		
21·2	Insurance – liability etc. of Employer		
21·3	Excepted Risks		
22	**Insurance of the Works**		*37*
22·1	Insurance of the Works – alternative clauses		
22·2	Definitions		
22·3	Nominated and Domestic Sub-Contractors – benefit of Joint Names Policies – Specified Perils		
22A	**Erection of new buildings – All Risks Insurance of the Works by the Contractor**		*39*
22A·1	New buildings – Contractor to take out and maintain a Joint Names Policy for All Risks Insurance		
22A·2	Single policy – insurers approved by Employer – failure by Contractor to insure		
22A·3	Use of annual policy maintained by Contractor – alternative to use of clause 22A·2		
22A·4	Loss or damage to Works – insurance claims – Contractor's obligations – use of insurance monies		
22A·5	·1 Terrorism cover – non-availability		
	·2 Employer's options		
	·4 Premium rate changes – terrorism cover		
22B	**Erection of new buildings – All Risks Insurance of the Works by the Employer**		*41*
22B·1	New buildings – Employer to take out and maintain a Joint Names Policy for All Risks Insurance		
22B·2	Failure of Employer to insure – rights of Contractor		
22B·3	Loss or damage to Works – insurance claims – Contractor's obligations – payment by Employer		
22B·4	·1 Terrorism cover – non-availability		
	·2 Employer's options		
22C	**Insurance of existing structures – insurance of Works in or extensions to existing structures**		*42*
22C·1	Existing structures and contents – Specified Perils – Employer to take out and maintain Joint Names Policy		
22C·1A	Terrorism cover – existing structures and contents – non-availability – Employer's options		
22C·2	Works in or extensions to existing structures – All Risks Insurance – Employer to take out and maintain Joint Names Policy		
22C·3	Failure of Employer to insure – rights of Contractor		
22C·4	Loss or damage to Works – insurance claims – Contractor's obligations – payment by Employer		
22C·5	·1 Terrorism cover – non-availability		
	·2 Employer's options		
22D	**Insurance for Employer's loss of liquidated damages – clause 25·4·3**		*45*
22FC	**Joint Fire Code – compliance**		*46*
	·1 Application of clause		
	·2 Compliance with Joint Fire Code		
	·3 Breach of Joint Fire Code – Remedial Measures		
	·4 Indemnity		
	·5 Joint Fire Code – amendments		
23	**Date of Possession, completion and postponement**		*46*
23·1	Date of Possession – progress to Completion Date		
23·2	Architect's instructions – postponement		
23·3	Possession by Contractor – use or occupation by Employer		
24	**Damages for non-completion**		*47*
24·1	Certificate of Architect		
24·2	Payment or allowance of liquidated damages		
25	**Extension of time**		*48*
25·1	Interpretation of delay		
25·2	Notice by Contractor of delay to progress		
25·3	Fixing Completion Date		
25·4	Relevant Events		
26	**Loss and expense caused by matters materially affecting regular progress of the Works**		*51*
26·1	Matters materially affecting regular progress of the Works – direct loss and/or expense		
26·2	List of matters		
26·3	Relevance of certain extensions of Completion Date		
26·4	Nominated Sub-Contractors – matters materially affecting regular progress of the sub-contract works – direct loss and/or expense		
26·5	Amounts ascertained – added to Contract Sum		
26·6	Reservation of rights and remedies of Contractor		
27	**Determination by Employer**		*53*
27·1	Notices under clause 27		
27·2	Default by Contractor		
27·3	Insolvency of Contractor		
27·4	Corruption		
27·5	Insolvency of Contractor – option to Employer		
27·6	Consequences of determination under clauses 27·2 to 27·4		
27·7	Employer decides not to complete the Works		
27·8	Other rights and remedies		
28	**Determination by Contractor**		*57*
28·1	Notices under clause 28		
28·2	Default by Employer – suspension of uncompleted Works		
28·3	Insolvency of Employer		
28·4	Consequences of determination under clause 28·2 or 28·3		
28·5	Other rights and remedies		
28A	**Determination by Employer or Contractor**		*59*
28A·1	Grounds for determination of the employment of the Contractor		
28A·2/ 28A·6	Consequences of determination under clause 28A·1·1 – clauses 28A·3 to 28A·6		
28A·7	Amounts attributable to any Nominated Sub-Contractor		

29	**Works by Employer or persons employed or engaged by Employer**	61			**Payment of Nominated Sub-Contractor**	76
29·1	Information in Contract Bills		35·13	·1	Architect – direction as to interim	
29·2	Information not in Contract Bills		and ·2		payment for Nominated Sub-Contractor	
				·3	Direct payment of Nominated Sub-	
30	**Certificates and payments**	61	to ·5		Contractor	
30A	Payments subject to clause 31			·6	Agreement NSC/W – pre-nomination payments to Nominated Sub-Contractor by Employer	
30·1	·1·1 Interim Certificates and valuations –					
to ·1·5	final date for payment – interest					
	·1·6 Advance payment		35·14		**Extension of period or periods for completion of nominated sub-contract works**	77
	·2·1 Interim valuations					
	·2·2 Application by Contractor – amount of gross valuation		35·15		**Failure to complete nominated sub-contract works**	77
	·3 Issue of Interim Certificates					
	·4 Right of suspension of obligations by Contractor		35·16		**Practical completion of nominated sub-contract works**	78
30·2	Ascertainment of amounts due in Interim Certificates					
30·3	Off-site materials or goods – the 'listed items'		35·17 to ·19		**Early final payment of Nominated Sub-Contractors**	78
30·4	Retention – rules for ascertainment					
30·4A	Contractor's bond in lieu of Retention		35·17			
30·5	Rules on treatment of Retention		35·18		Defects in nominated sub-contract works after final payment of Nominated Sub-Contractor – before issue of Final Certificate	
30·6	·1 Final adjustment of Contract Sum – documents from Contractor					
	·2 Items included in adjustment of Contract Sum		35·19		Final payment – saving provisions	
30·7	Interim Certificate – final adjustment or ascertainment of nominated sub-contract sums		35·20		**Position of Employer in relation to Nominated Sub-Contractor**	79
30·8	Issue of Final Certificate					
30·9	Effect of Final Certificate		35·21		**Clause 2·1 of Agreement NSC/W – position of Contractor**	79
30·10	Effect of certificates other than Final Certificate					
31	**Construction Industry Scheme (CIS)**	70	35·22		**Restrictions in contracts of sale etc. – limitation of liability of Nominated Sub-Contractors**	79
31·1	Definitions					
31·2	Whether Employer is a 'contractor'					
31·3	Payment by Employer – valid Authorisation essential		35·23		[Number not used]	79
31·4	Validity of Authorisation – Employer's query		35·24		**Circumstances where re-nomination necessary**	79
31·5	Authorisation: CIS 4 registration card					
31·6	Authorisation: CIS 5 or CIS 6 or a certifying document		35·25 and 35·26		**Determination or determination of employment of Nominated Sub-Contractor – Architect's instructions**	81
31·7	Change of Authorisation					
31·10	Vouchers					
31·12	Correction of errors in making the statutory deduction		**36**		**NOMINATED SUPPLIERS**	82
			36·1		Definition of a Nominated Supplier	
31·13	Relation to other clauses		36·2		Architect's instructions	
31·14	Disputes or differences		36·3		Ascertainment of costs to be set against prime cost sum	
32	[Number not used]	72	36·4		Sale contract provisions – Architect's right to nominate supplier	
33	[Number not used]	72	36·5		Contract of sale – restriction, limitation or exclusion of liability	
34	**Antiquities**	72				
34·1	Effect of find of antiquities				**CONDITIONS: PART 3: FLUCTUATIONS**	
34·2	Architect's instructions on antiquities found					
34·3	Direct loss and/or expense					
	CONDITIONS: PART 2: NOMINATED SUB-CONTRACTORS AND NOMINATED SUPPLIERS		**37**		**Choice of fluctuation provisions – entry in Appendix**	85
					Note: Clauses 38, 39 and 40 are published separately	
35	**NOMINATED SUB-CONTRACTORS**	73				
	General	73	**38**		**CONTRIBUTION, LEVY AND TAX FLUCTUATIONS**	
35·1	Definition of a Nominated Sub-Contractor					
35·2	Contractor's tender for works otherwise reserved for a Nominated Sub-Contractor		38·1	·1	Deemed calculation of Contract Sum – types and rates of contribution etc.	
				·2	Increases or decreases in rates of contribution etc. – payment or allowance	
	Procedure for nomination of a sub-contractor	73		·3	Persons employed on site other than	
35·3			and ·4		'workpeople'	
35·4	Documents relating to Nominated Sub-Contractors			·5/·7	Refunds and premiums	
				·8	Contracted-out employment	
35·5	Contractor's right of reasonable objection			·9	Meaning of contribution etc.	
35·6	Architect's instruction on Nomination NSC/N		38·2		Materials – duties and taxes	
35·7	Contractor's obligations on receipt of Architect's instruction		38·3		**Fluctuations – work sub-let – Domestic Sub-Contractors**	
35·8	Non-compliance with clause 35·7 – Contractor's obligation to notify Architect		38·3	·1	Sub-let work – incorporation of provisions to like effect	
35·9	Architect's duty on receipt of any notice under clause 35·8		38·3	·2	Sub-let work – fluctuations – payment to or allowance by the Contractor	
35·10	[Number not used]					
35·11	[Number not used]					
35·12	[Number not used]					

38·4 to ·6		**Provisions relating to clause 38**		41A·7	Effect of Adjudicator's decision
38·4	·1	Written notice by Contractor		41A·8	Immunity
	·2	Timing and effect of written notices		**41B**	**Arbitration** 88
	·3	Agreement – Quantity Surveyor and Contractor		**41C**	**Legal proceedings** 89
	·4	Fluctuations added to or deducted from Contract Sum			**CONDITIONS: PART 5: PERFORMANCE SPECIFIED WORK** 90
	·5	Evidence and computations by Contractor		42·1	Meaning of Performance Specified Work
	·6	No alteration to Contractor's profit		42·2	Contractor's Statement
	·7	Position where Contractor in default		42·3	Contents of Contractor's Statement
and	·8	over completion		42·4	Time for Contractor's Statement
38·5		Work etc. to which clauses 38·1 to ·3 not applicable		42·5	Architect's notice to amend Contractor's Statement
38·6		Definitions for use with clause 38		42·6	Architect's notice of deficiency in Contractor's Statement
38·7		**Percentage addition to fluctuation payments or allowances**		42·7	Definition of provisional sum for Performance Specified Work
39		**LABOUR AND MATERIALS COST AND TAX FLUCTUATIONS**		42·8	Instructions of the Architect on other provisional sums
39·1	·1	Deemed calculation of Contract Sum – rates of wages etc.		42·9	Preparation of Contract Bills
	·2	Increases or decreases in rates of wages etc. – payment or allowance		42·10	Provisional sum for Performance Specified Work – errors or omissions in Contract Bills
	·3	Persons employed on site other than		42·11	Variations in respect of Performance Specified Work
and	·4	'workpeople'		42·12	Agreement for additional Performance Specified Work
	·5	Workpeople – wage-fixing body –		42·13	Analysis
and	·6	reimbursement of fares		42·14	Integration of Performance Specified Work
39·2		Contributions, levies and taxes		42·15	Compliance with Architect's instructions – Contractor's notice of injurious affection
39·3		Materials, goods, electricity and fuels		42·16	Delay by Contractor in providing the Contractor's Statement
39·4		**Fluctuations – work sub-let – Domestic Sub-Contractors**		42·17	Performance Specified Work – Contractor's obligation
39·4	·1	Sub-let work – incorporation of provisions to like effect		42·18	Nomination excluded
	·2	Sub-let work – fluctuations – payment to or allowance by the Contractor			**CODE OF PRACTICE: REFERRED TO IN CLAUSE 8·4·4** 93
39·5 to ·7		**Provisions relating to clause 39**			**APPENDIX** 94
39·5	·1	Written notice by Contractor			**ANNEX 1 TO APPENDIX: TERMS OF BONDS** 98
	·2	Timing and effect of written notices			Advance Payment Bond
	·3	Agreement – Quantity Surveyor and Contractor			Bond in respect of payment for off-site materials and/or goods
	·4	Fluctuations added to or deducted from Contract Sum			**SUPPLEMENTAL PROVISIONS (the VAT Agreement)** 104
	·5	Evidence and computations by Contractor		1	Interim payments – addition of VAT
	·6	No alteration to Contractor's profit		1A	Alternative provisions to clauses 1·1 to 1·2·2 inclusive
	·7	Position where Contractor in default		1·1	Written assessment by Contractor
and	·8	over completion		1·2	Employer to calculate amount of tax due – Employer's right of reasonable objection
39·6		Work etc. to which clauses 39·1 to ·4 not applicable		1·3	Written final statement – VAT liability of Contractor – recovery from Employer
39·7		Definitions for use with clause 39		1·4	Contractor to issue receipt as tax invoice
39·8		**Percentage addition to fluctuation payments or allowances**		2	Value of supply – liquidated damages to be disregarded
40		**USE OF PRICE ADJUSTMENT FORMULAE**		3	Employer's right to challenge tax claimed by Contractor
40·1		Adjustment of Contract Sum – price adjustment formulae for building contracts – Formula Rules		4	Discharge of Employer from liability to pay tax to the Contractor
40·2		Amendment to clause 30 – interim valuations		5	Awards in dispute procedures
40·3		Fluctuations – articles manufactured outside the United Kingdom		6	Arbitration provision excluded
40·4		[Number not used]		7	Employer's right where receipt not provided
40·5		Power to agree – Quantity Surveyor and Contractor		8	VAT on determination
40·6		Position where Monthly Bulletins are delayed, etc.			**ANNEX 2 TO THE CONDITIONS: Supplemental Provisions for EDI** 108
40·7		Formula adjustment – failure to complete			**ANNEX 3 TO THE CONDITIONS: Bond in lieu of Retention** 109
		CONDITIONS: PART 4: SETTLEMENT OF DISPUTES – ADJUDICATION – ARBITRATION – LEGAL PROCEEDINGS			List of amendments incorporated in this reprint 112
41A		**Adjudication** 86			
41A·1		Application of clause 41A			
41A·2		Identity of Adjudicator			
41A·3		Death of Adjudicator – inability to adjudicate			
41A·4		Dispute or difference – notice of intention to refer to adjudication – referral			
41A·5		Conduct of the adjudication			
41A·6		Adjudicator's fee and reasonable expenses – payment			

Articles of Agreement

made the _____ day of _____ 20 _____

BETWEEN _____

_____

of (or whose registered office is situated at) _____

_____

_____

(hereinafter called 'the Employer') of the one part

AND _____

_____

of (or whose registered office is situated at) _____

_____

_____

(hereinafter called 'the Contractor') [a] of the other part.

Footnote

[a] Where the Contractor is not a limited liability company incorporated under the Companies Acts, see footnote [qq] to clause 35·13·5·3·4.

Whereas

Recitals

First the Employer is desirous of [b] _____

_____

_____

at _____

_____

and has caused Drawings and Bills of Quantities to be prepared which show and describe the work to be done;

Second the Contractor has supplied the Employer with a fully priced copy of the said Bills of Quantities (which copy is hereinafter referred to as 'the Contract Bills');

[e] and has provided the Employer with a priced Activity Schedule;

Third the said Drawings numbered _____

_____

(hereinafter referred to as 'the Contract Drawings') and the Contract Bills have been signed by or on behalf of the parties hereto;

Fourth the status of the Employer, for the purposes of the Construction Industry Scheme (CIS) under the Income and Corporation Taxes Act 1988 or any statutory amendment or modification thereof, as at the Base Date is stated in the Appendix;

[f] Fifth the extent of the application of the Construction (Design and Management) Regulations 1994 (the 'CDM Regulations') to the work referred to in the First recital is stated in the Appendix;

[e] Sixth the Employer has provided the Contractor with a schedule ('Information Release Schedule') which states what information the Architect will release and the time of that release;

Seventh if the Employer requires any bond to be on terms other than those agreed between the JCT and the British Bankers' Association, the Contractor has been given copies of these terms;

Footnotes

[b] State nature of intended works.

[c] [d] Not used.

[e] Delete if not provided.

[f] See the notes on the JCT 80 Fifth recital in Practice Note 27 'The application of the Construction (Design and Management) Regulations 1994 to Contracts on JCT Standard Forms of Contract' for the statutory obligations which must have been fulfilled before the Contractor can begin carrying out the Works.

Now it is hereby agreed as follows

Contractor's obligations

Article 1
For the consideration hereinafter mentioned the Contractor will upon and subject to the Contract Documents carry out and complete the Works shown upon, described by or referred to in those Documents.

Contract Sum

Article 2
The Employer will pay to the Contractor the sum of _____

_____

_____(£_____ . _____)
(hereinafter referred to as 'the Contract Sum') or such other sum as shall become payable hereunder at the times and in the manner specified in the Conditions.

Architect

Article 3
The term 'the Architect' in the Conditions shall mean

_____

of _____

_____

or, in the event of his death or ceasing to be the Architect for the purpose of this Contract, such other person as the Employer shall nominate within a reasonable time but in any case no later than 21 days after such death or cessation for that purpose, not being a person to whom the Contractor no later than 7 days after such nomination shall object for reasons considered to be sufficient by a person appointed pursuant to the procedures under this Contract relevant to the resolution of disputes or differences. Provided always that no person subsequently appointed to be the Architect under this Contract shall be entitled to disregard or overrule any certificate or opinion or decision or approval or instruction given or expressed by the Architect for the time being.

Footnotes [g] [h] [i] Not used.

Quantity Surveyor

Article 4
The term 'the Quantity Surveyor' in the Conditions shall mean

_____

of _____

_____

or, in the event of his death or ceasing to be the Quantity Surveyor for the purpose of this Contract, such other person as the Employer shall nominate within a reasonable time but in any case no later than 21 days after such death or cessation for that purpose, not being a person to whom the Contractor no later than 7 days after such nomination shall object for reasons considered to be sufficient by a person appointed pursuant to the procedures under this Contract relevant to the resolution of disputes or differences.

Dispute or difference – adjudication

Article 5
If any dispute or difference arises under this Contract either Party may refer it to adjudication in accordance with clause 41A.

Planning Supervisor

Article 6·1 [k]
The term 'the Planning Supervisor' in the Conditions shall mean the Architect

or _____

of _____

_____

or in the event of the death of the Planning Supervisor or his ceasing to be the Planning Supervisor such other person as the Employer shall appoint as the Planning Supervisor pursuant to regulation 6(5) of the CDM Regulations.

Principal Contractor

Article 6·2 [k]
The term 'the Principal Contractor' in the Conditions shall mean the Contractor, or, in the event of his ceasing to be the Principal Contractor, such other contractor as the Employer shall appoint as the Principal Contractor pursuant to regulation 6(5) of the CDM Regulations.

Footnotes

[j] Not used.

[k] Delete articles 6·1 and 6·2 when only regulations 7 and 13 of the CDM Regulations apply; see Appendix under the reference to the Fifth recital.

Dispute or difference – arbitration

Article 7A
Where the entry in the Appendix stating that "Clause 41B applies" has not been deleted then, subject to article 5, if any dispute or difference as to any matter or thing of whatsoever nature arising under this Contract or in connection therewith, except in connection with the enforcement of any decision of an Adjudicator appointed to determine a dispute or difference arising thereunder, shall arise between the Parties either during the progress or after the completion or abandonment of the Works or after the determination of the employment of the Contractor, except under clause 31 *(Construction Industry Scheme)* to the extent provided in clause 31·14 or under clause 3 of the VAT Agreement, it shall be referred to arbitration in accordance with clause 41B and the JCT 1998 edition of the Construction Industry Model Arbitration Rules (CIMAR). [l]

Dispute or difference – legal proceedings

Article 7B
Where the entry in the Appendix stating that "Clause 41B applies" has been deleted then, subject to article 5, if any dispute or difference as to any matter or thing of whatsoever nature arising under this Contract or in connection therewith shall arise between the Parties either during the progress or after the completion or abandonment of the Works or after the determination of the employment of the Contractor it shall be determined by legal proceedings.

Footnotes

[l] The JCT 1998 edition of the Construction Industry Model Arbitration Rules (CIMAR) contains procedures for beginning an arbitration and the appointment of an arbitrator, the consolidation or joinder of disputes including related disputes between different parties engaged under different contracts on the same project, and for the conduct of arbitral proceedings. The objective of CIMAR is the fair, impartial, speedy, cost-effective and binding resolution of construction disputes. The JCT 1998 edition of the Construction Industry Model Arbitration Rules (CIMAR) includes additional rules concerning the calling of preliminary meetings and supplemental and advisory procedures which may, with the agreement of the parties, be used with Rule 7 (short hearing), 8 (documents only) or 9 (full procedure).

[m] Not used.

Notes	
[A1] For Agreement executed under hand and NOT as a deed.	**[A1] AS WITNESS THE HANDS OF THE PARTIES HERETO**

[A1] Signed by or on behalf of the Employer _____

      in the presence of:

[A1] Signed by or on behalf of the Contractor _____

      in the presence of: |

– –

[A2] For Agreement executed as a deed under the law of England and Wales by a company or other body corporate: insert the name of the party mentioned and identified on page 1 and then use *either* [A3] and [A4] *or* [A5]. If the party is an *individual* see note [A6].

[A3] For use if the party is using its common seal, which should be affixed under the party's name.

[A4] For use of the party's officers authorised to affix its common seal. | **[A2] EXECUTED AS A DEED BY THE EMPLOYER**
      hereinbefore mentioned namely _____

[A3]   by affixing hereto its common seal

[A4]   in the presence of: |

*   OR –

[A5] For use if the party is a company registered under the Companies Acts which is not using a common seal: insert the names of the two officers by whom the company is acting *who MUST be either a director and the company secretary or two directors*, and insert their signatures with 'Director' or 'Secretary' as appropriate. *This method of execution is NOT valid for local authorities or certain other bodies incorporated by Act of Parliament or by charter if exempted under s.718(2) of the Companies Act 1985.*	[A5] acting by a director and its secretary*/two directors* whose signatures are here subscribed:
namely _____

[Signature] _____ DIRECTOR

and _____

[Signature] _____ SECRETARY*/DIRECTOR*

[A2] AND AS A DEED BY THE CONTRACTOR
      hereinbefore mentioned namely _____

[A3]   by affixing hereto its common seal

[A4]   in the presence of: |

[A6] If executed as a deed by an *individual*: insert the name at [A2], delete the words at [A3], substitute 'whose signature is here subscribed' and insert the individual's signature. The individual MUST sign in the presence of a witness who attests the signature. Insert at [A4] the signature and name of the witness. Sealing by an individual is not required.

Other attestation clauses are required under the law of Scotland.

* *Delete as appropriate* | *   OR –

[A5]   acting by a director and its secretary*/two directors* whose signatures are here subscribed:
namely _____

[Signature] _____ DIRECTOR

and _____

[Signature] _____ SECRETARY*/DIRECTOR* |

P With 98 (9/03)   © The Joint Contracts Tribunal Limited 2003

The Conditions

Part 1: General

1 **Interpretation, definitions etc.**

Method of reference to clauses

1·1 Unless otherwise specifically stated a reference in the Articles of Agreement, the Conditions or the Appendix to any clause means that clause of the Conditions.

Articles etc. to be read as a whole

1·2 The Articles of Agreement, the Conditions and the Appendix are to be read as a whole and the effect or operation of any article or clause in the Conditions or item in or entry in the Appendix must therefore unless otherwise specifically stated be read subject to any relevant qualification or modification in any other article or any of the clauses in the Conditions or item in or entry in the Appendix.

Definitions

1·3 Unless the context otherwise requires or the Articles or the Conditions or an item in or entry in the Appendix specifically otherwise provides, the following words and phrases in the Articles of Agreement, the Conditions and the Appendix shall have the meanings given below or as ascribed in the article, clause or Appendix item to which reference is made:

Word or phrase	*Meaning*
3·3A Quotation:	a Quotation by a Nominated Sub-Contractor pursuant to **clause 3·3A** of Conditions NSC/C *(Conditions of Nominated Sub-Contract)*.
13A Quotation:	see **clause 13A·1·1**.
Activity Schedule:	the schedule of activities as attached to the Appendix with each activity priced and with the sum of those prices being the Contract Sum excluding provisional sums, prime cost sums and any Contractor's profit thereon and the value of work for which Approximate Quantities are included in the Contract Bills: see **clause 30·2·1**.
Adjudication Agreement:	see **clause 41A·2·1**.
Adjudicator:	any individual appointed pursuant to **clause 41A** as the Adjudicator.
All Risks Insurance:	see **clause 22·2**.
Analysis:	see **clause 42·13**.
Appendix:	the Appendix to the Conditions as completed by the parties.
Approximate Quantity:	a quantity in the Contract Bills identified therein as an approximate quantity.
Arbitrator:	the person appointed under **clause 41B** to be the Arbitrator.
Architect:	the person entitled to the use of the name 'Architect' and named in **article 3** or any successor duly appointed under **article 3** or otherwise agreed as the person to be the Architect.
Articles or Articles of Agreement:	the Articles of Agreement to which the Conditions are annexed, and references to any recital are to the recitals set out before the Articles.
Base Date:	the date stated in the **Appendix**.

Footnote [n] [Not used].

Word or phrase	Meaning
CDM Regulations:	the Construction (Design and Management) Regulations 1994 or any remaking thereof or any amendment to a regulation therein.
Certificate of Completion of Making Good Defects:	see **clause 17·4**.
Completion Date:	the Date for Completion as fixed and stated in the **Appendix** or any date fixed either under **clause 25** or in a confirmed acceptance of a 13A Quotation.
Conditions:	the clauses 1 to 37, either clause 38 or 39 or 40, clauses 41A, 41B, 41C and 42 and the Supplemental Provisions ('the VAT Agreement') annexed to the Articles of Agreement.
confirmed acceptance:	see **clause 13A·3·2**.
Contract Bills:	the Bills of Quantities referred to in the **First recital** which have been priced by the Contractor and signed by or on behalf of the Parties to this Contract.
Contract Documents:	the Contract Drawings, the Contract Bills, the Articles of Agreement, the Conditions and the Appendix.
Contract Drawings:	the Drawings referred to in the **First recital** which have been signed by or on behalf of the Parties to this Contract.
Contract Sum:	the sum named in **article 2** but subject to **clause 15·2**.
Contractor:	the person named as Contractor in the Articles of Agreement.
Contractor's Statement:	see **clause 42**.
Date for Completion:	the date fixed and stated in the **Appendix**.
Date of Possession:	the date stated in the **Appendix** under the reference to **clause 23·1**.
Defects Liability Period:	the period named in the **Appendix** under the reference to **clause 17·2**.
Domestic Sub-Contractor:	see **clause 19·2**.
Employer:	the person named as Employer in the Articles of Agreement.
Excepted Risks:	ionising radiations or contamination by radioactivity from any nuclear fuel or from any nuclear waste from the combustion of nuclear fuel, radioactive toxic explosive or other hazardous properties of any explosive nuclear assembly or nuclear component thereof, pressure waves caused by aircraft or other aerial devices travelling at sonic or supersonic speeds.
Final Certificate:	the certificate to which **clause 30·8** refers.
Health and Safety Plan:	where it is stated in the Appendix that all the CDM Regulations apply, the plan provided to the Principal Contractor and developed by him to comply with regulation 15(4) of the CDM Regulations and, for the purpose of regulation 10 of the CDM Regulations, received by the Employer before any construction work under this Contract has started; and any further development of that plan by the Principal Contractor during the progress of the Works.

Word or phrase	Meaning
Information Release Schedule:	the schedule referred to in the **Sixth recital** or as varied pursuant to **clause 5·4·1**.
Interim Certificate:	any one of the certificates to which **clauses 30·1** and **30·7** and the entry in the **Appendix** under the reference to **clause 30·1·3** refer.
Joint Fire Code:	the Joint Code of Practice on the Protection from Fire of Construction Sites and Buildings Undergoing Renovation which is published by the Construction Confederation and the Fire Protection Association with the support of the Association of British Insurers, the Chief and Assistant Chief Fire Officers Association and the London Fire Brigade which is current at the Base Date, and as may be amended/revised from time to time.
Joint Names Policy:	see **clause 22·2**.
Nominated Sub-Contract:	an Agreement NSC/A *(Articles of Nominated Sub-Contract Agreement)*, the Conditions NSC/C *(Conditions of Nominated Sub-Contract)* incorporated therein and the documents annexed thereto.
Nominated Sub-Contractor:	see **clause 35·1**.
Nominated Supplier:	see **clause 36·1·1**.
Numbered Documents:	the Numbered Documents annexed to Agreement NSC/A *(Articles of Nominated Sub-Contract Agreement)*.
Parties:	the Employer and the Contractor named as the Employer and the Contractor in the Articles of Agreement.
Party:	the Employer or the Contractor named as the Employer or the Contractor in the Articles of Agreement.
Performance Specified Work:	see **clause 42·1**.
Period of Interim Certificates:	the period named in the **Appendix** under the reference to **clause 30·1·3**.
person:	an individual, firm (partnership) or body corporate.
Planning Supervisor:	the Architect or the other person named in **article 6·1** or any successor duly appointed by the Employer as the Planning Supervisor pursuant to regulation 6(5) of the CDM Regulations.
Practical Completion:	see **clause 17·1**.
Price Statement:	see **clause 13·4·1·2 Alternative A**.
Principal Contractor:	the Contractor or any other contractor duly appointed by the Employer as the Principal Contractor pursuant to regulation 6(5) of the CDM Regulations.
provisional sum:	includes a sum provided for work whether or not identified as being for defined or undefined work and a provisional sum for Performance Specified Work: see **clause 42·7**.
Public Holiday:	Christmas Day, Good Friday or a day which under the Banking and Financial Dealings Act 1971 is a bank holiday. [o]

Footnote [o] Amend as necessary if different Public Holidays are applicable.

Word or phrase	Meaning
Quantity Surveyor:	the person named in **article 4** or any successor duly appointed under **article 4** or otherwise agreed as the person to be the Quantity Surveyor.
Relevant Event:	any one of the events set out in **clause 25·4**.
Retention:	see **clause 30·2**.
Retention Percentage:	see **clause 30·4·1·1** and any entry in the **Appendix** under the reference to **clause 30·4·1·1**.
Site Materials:	all unfixed materials and goods delivered to, placed on or adjacent to the Works and intended for incorporation therein.
Specified Perils:	fire, lightning, explosion, storm, tempest, flood, bursting or overflowing of water tanks, apparatus or pipes, earthquake, aircraft and other aerial devices or articles dropped therefrom, riot and civil commotion, but excluding Excepted Risks.
Standard Method of Measurement:	the Standard Method of Measurement of Building Works, 7th Edition, published by The Royal Institution of Chartered Surveyors and the Construction Confederation current, unless otherwise stated in the Contract Bills, at the Base Date.
Statutory Requirements:	see **clause 6·1·1**.
Valuation:	a valuation by the Quantity Surveyor pursuant to **clause 13·4·1·2 Alternative B** or the amount of any Price Statement or any part thereof accepted pursuant to **clause 13·4·1·2 paragraph A2** or amended Price Statement or any part thereof accepted pursuant to **clause 13·4·1·2 paragraph A4·2**.
Variation:	see **clause 13·1**.
VAT Agreement:	see **clause 15·1**.
Works:	the works briefly described in the **First recital** and shown upon, described by or referred to in the Contract Documents and including any changes made to these works in accordance with this Contract.

1·4 [Number not used]

Contractor's responsibility

1·5 Notwithstanding any obligation of the Architect to the Employer and whether or not the Employer appoints a clerk of works, the Contractor shall remain wholly responsible for carrying out and completing the Works in all respects in accordance with the Conditions, whether or not the Architect or the clerk of works, if appointed, at any time goes on to the Works or to any workshop or other place where work is being prepared to inspect the same or otherwise, or the Architect includes the value of any work, materials or goods in a certificate for payment or issues the certificate of Practical Completion or the Certificate of Completion of Making Good Defects.

Reappointment of Planning Supervisor or Principal Contractor – notification to Contractor

1·6 If the Employer pursuant to article 6·1 or to article 6·2 by a further appointment replaces the Planning Supervisor referred to in, or appointed pursuant to, article 6·1 or replaces the Contractor or any other contractor appointed as the Principal Contractor, the Employer shall immediately upon such further appointment notify the Contractor in writing of the name and address of the new appointee.

Giving or service of notices or other documents	1·7		Where the Contract does not specifically state the manner of giving or service of any notice or other document required or authorised in pursuance of this Contract such notice or other document shall be given or served by any effective means to any agreed address. If no address has been agreed then if given or served by being addressed, pre-paid and delivered by post to the addressee's last known principal business address or, where the addressee is a body corporate, to the body's registered or principal office it shall be treated as having been effectively given or served.
Reckoning periods of days	1·8		Where under this Contract an act is required to be done within a specified period of days after or from a specified date, the period shall begin immediately after that date. Where the period would include a day which is a Public Holiday that day shall be excluded.
Employer's Representative	1·9		The Employer may give written notice to the Contractor that from the date stated in the notice the individual identified in the notice will exercise all the functions ascribed to the Employer in the Conditions subject to any exceptions stated in the notice. [p]
Applicable law	1·10		Whatever the nationality, residence or domicile of the Employer, the Contractor or any sub-contractor or supplier and wherever the Works are situated the law of England shall be the law applicable to this Contract. [q]
Electronic data interchange	1·11		Where the Appendix so states, the 'Supplemental Provisions for EDI' annexed to the Conditions shall apply.
Contracts (Rights of Third Parties) Act 1999 – contracting out	1·12		Notwithstanding any other provision of this Contract nothing in this Contract confers or purports to confer any right to enforce any of its terms on any person who is not a party to it.

2 Contractor's obligations

Contract Documents	2·1		The Contractor shall upon and subject to the Conditions carry out and complete the Works in compliance with the Contract Documents, using materials and workmanship of the quality and standards therein specified, provided that where and to the extent that approval of the quality of materials or of the standards of workmanship is a matter for the opinion of the Architect such quality and standards shall be to the reasonable satisfaction of the Architect.
Contract Bills – relation to Articles, Conditions and Appendix	2·2	·1	Nothing contained in the Contract Bills shall override or modify the application or interpretation of that which is contained in the Articles of Agreement, the Conditions or the Appendix.
	2·2	·2	Subject always to clause 2·2·1:
Preparation of Contract Bills – errors in preparation etc.		·2 ·1	the Contract Bills (or any addendum bill issued as part of the information referred to in clause 13A·1·1 for the purpose of obtaining a 13A Quotation), unless otherwise specifically stated therein in respect of any specified item or items, are to have been prepared in accordance with the Standard Method of Measurement;
		·2 ·2	if in the Contract Bills (or in any addendum bill issued as part of the information referred to in clause 13A·1·1 for the purpose of obtaining a 13A Quotation which Quotation has been accepted by the Employer) there is any departure from the method of preparation referred to in clause 2·2·2·1 or any error in description or in quantity or omission of items (including any error in or omission of information in any item which is the subject of a provisional sum for defined work) then such departure or error or omission shall not vitiate this Contract but the departure or error or omission shall be corrected; where the description of a provisional sum for defined work does not provide the information required by the Standard Method of Measurement the correction shall be made by correcting the description so that it does provide such information; any such correction under this clause 2·2·2·2 shall be treated as if it were a Variation required by an instruction of the Architect under clause 13·2.
Discrepancies in or divergences between documents	2·3		If the Contractor shall find any discrepancy in or divergence between any two or more of the following documents, including a divergence between parts of any one of them or between documents of the same description, namely:

Footnotes

[p] To avoid any possible confusion over the quite distinct roles of the Architect and Quantity Surveyor and the role of the Employer's Representative neither the Architect nor the Quantity Surveyor should be appointed as the Employer's Representative.

[q] Where the Parties do not wish the law applicable to this Contract to be the law of England appropriate amendments to clause 1·10 should be made.

2·3 ·1 the Contract Drawings,

2·3 ·2 the Contract Bills,

2·3 ·3 any instruction issued by the Architect under the Conditions (save insofar as any such instruction requires a Variation in accordance with the provisions of clause 13·2),

2·3 ·4 any drawings or documents issued by the Architect under clause 5·3·1·1, 5·4·1, 5·4·2 or 7, and

2·3 ·5 the Numbered Documents,

he shall immediately give to the Architect a written notice specifying the discrepancy or divergence, and the Architect shall issue instructions in regard thereto.

2·4 ·1 If the Contractor shall find any discrepancy or divergence between his Statement in respect of Performance Specified Work and any instruction of the Architect issued after receipt by the Architect of the Contractor's Statement, he shall immediately give to the Architect a written notice specifying the discrepancy or divergence, and the Architect shall issue instructions in regard thereto.

2·4 ·2 If the Contractor or the Architect shall find any discrepancy in the Contractor's Statement, the Contractor shall correct the Statement to remove the discrepancy and inform the Architect in writing of the correction made. Such correction shall be at no cost to the Employer.

3 Contract Sum – additions or deductions – adjustment – Interim Certificates

Where in the Conditions it is provided that an amount is to be added to or deducted from the Contract Sum or dealt with by adjustment of the Contract Sum then as soon as such amount is ascertained in whole or in part such amount shall be taken into account in the computation of the next Interim Certificate following such whole or partial ascertainment.

4 Architect's instructions

Compliance with Architect's instructions

4·1 ·1 The Contractor shall forthwith comply with all instructions issued to him by the Architect in regard to any matter in respect of which the Architect is expressly empowered by the Conditions to issue instructions; save that:

·1 ·1 where such instruction is one requiring a Variation within the meaning of clause 13·1·2 the Contractor need not comply to the extent that he makes reasonable objection in writing to the Architect to such compliance;

·1 ·2 where pursuant to clause 13·2·3 clause 13A applies to an instruction, the Variation to which that instruction refers shall not be carried out until

– the Architect has issued to the Contractor a confirmed acceptance of the 13A Quotation

or

– an instruction in respect of the Variation has been issued under clause 13A·4·1.

4·1 ·2 If within 7 days after receipt of a written notice from the Architect requiring compliance with an instruction the Contractor does not comply therewith, then the Employer may employ and pay other persons to execute any work whatsoever which may be necessary to give effect to such instruction; and all costs incurred in connection with such employment may be deducted by him from any monies due or to become due to the Contractor under this Contract or may be recoverable from the Contractor by the Employer as a debt.

Provisions empowering instructions

4·2 Upon receipt of what purports to be an instruction issued to him by the Architect the Contractor may request the Architect to specify in writing the provision of the Conditions which empowers the issue of the said instruction. The Architect shall forthwith comply with any such request, and if the Contractor shall thereafter comply with the said instruction (neither Party before such compliance having invoked the procedures under this Contract

4·2 *continued*

relevant to the resolution of disputes or differences in order that it may be decided whether the provision specified by the Architect empowers the issue of the said instruction), then the issue of the same shall be deemed for all the purposes of this Contract to have been empowered by the provision of the Conditions specified by the Architect in answer to the Contractor's request.

Instructions to be in writing

4·3 ·1 All instructions issued by the Architect shall be issued in writing.

Procedure if instructions given otherwise than in writing

4·3 ·2 If the Architect purports to issue an instruction otherwise than in writing it shall be of no immediate effect, but shall be confirmed in writing by the Contractor to the Architect within 7 days, and if not dissented from in writing by the Architect to the Contractor within 7 days from receipt of the Contractor's confirmation shall take effect as from the expiration of the latter said 7 days. Provided always:

·2 ·1 that if the Architect within 7 days of giving such an instruction otherwise than in writing shall himself confirm the same in writing, then the Contractor shall not be obliged to confirm as aforesaid, and the said instruction shall take effect as from the date of the Architect's confirmation; and

·2 ·2 that if neither the Contractor nor the Architect shall confirm such an instruction in the manner and at the time aforesaid but the Contractor shall nevertheless comply with the same, then the Architect may confirm the same in writing at any time prior to the issue of the Final Certificate, and the said instruction shall thereupon be deemed to have taken effect on the date on which it was issued otherwise than in writing by the Architect.

5 Contract Documents – other documents – issue of certificates

Custody of Contract Bills and Contract Drawings

5·1 The Contract Drawings and the Contract Bills shall remain in the custody of the Architect or the Quantity Surveyor so as to be available at all reasonable times for the inspection of the Employer and of the Contractor.

Copies of documents

5·2 Immediately after the execution of this Contract the Architect without charge to the Contractor shall provide him (unless he shall have been previously so provided) with:

5·2 ·1 one copy certified on behalf of the Employer of the Contract Documents;

5·2 ·2 two further copies of the Contract Drawings; and

5·2 ·3 two copies of the unpriced Bills of Quantities.

Descriptive schedules etc. – master programme of Contractor

5·3 ·1 So soon as is possible after the execution of this Contract:

·1 ·1 the Architect without charge to the Contractor shall provide him (unless he shall have been previously so provided) with 2 copies of any descriptive schedules or other like documents necessary for use in carrying out the Works; and

·1 ·2 the Contractor without charge to the Employer shall provide the Architect (unless he shall have been previously so provided) with 2 copies of his master programme for the execution of the Works and within 14 days of any decision by the Architect under clause 25·3·1 or of the date of issue of a confirmed acceptance of a 13A Quotation with 2 copies of any amendments and revisions to take account of that decision or of that confirmed acceptance. [r]

5·3 ·2 Nothing contained in the descriptive schedules or other like documents referred to in clause 5·3·1·1 (nor in the master programme for the execution of the Works or any amendment to that programme or revision therein referred to in clause 5·3·1·2) shall impose any obligation beyond those imposed by the Contract Documents. [s]

Information Release Schedule

5·4 ·1 Except to the extent that the Architect is prevented by the act or default of the Contractor or of any person for whom the Contractor is responsible, the Architect shall ensure that 2 copies of the information referred to in the Information Release Schedule are released at the time stated in the Schedule provided that the Employer and Contractor may agree, which agreement shall not be unreasonably delayed or withheld, to vary any such time.

Footnotes

[r] To be deleted if no master programme is required.

[s] Words in parentheses to be deleted if no master programme is required.

Provision of further drawings or details	5·4	·2	Except to the extent included in the Information Release Schedule the Architect as and when from time to time may be necessary without charge to the Contractor shall provide him with 2 copies of such further drawings or details which are reasonably necessary to explain and amplify the Contract Drawings and shall issue such instructions (including those for or in regard to the expenditure of provisional sums) to enable the Contractor to carry out and complete the Works in accordance with the Conditions. Such provision shall be made or instructions given at a time when, having regard to the progress of the Works, or, where in the opinion of the Architect Practical Completion of the Works is likely to be achieved before the Completion Date, having regard to such Completion Date, it was reasonably necessary for the Contractor to receive such further drawings or details or instructions. Where the Contractor is aware and has reasonable grounds for believing that the Architect is not so aware of the time when it is necessary for the Contractor to receive such further drawings or details or instructions the Contractor shall, if and to the extent that it is reasonably practicable to do so, advise the Architect of the time sufficiently in advance of when the Contractor needs such further drawings or details or instructions to enable the Architect to fulfil his obligations under clause 5·4·2.
Availability of certain documents	5·5		The Contractor shall keep one copy of the Contract Drawings, one copy of the unpriced Bills of Quantities, one copy of the descriptive schedules or other like documents referred to in clause 5·3·1·1, one copy of the master programme referred to in clause 5·3·1·2 (unless clause 5·3·1·2 has been deleted) and one copy of the drawings and details referred to in clause 5·4·2 upon the site so as to be available to the Architect or his representative at all reasonable times.
Return of drawings etc.	5·6		Upon final payment under clause 30·8 the Contractor shall if so requested by the Architect forthwith return to him all drawings, details, descriptive schedules and other documents of a like nature which bear the name of the Architect.
Limits to use of documents	5·7		None of the documents provided in accordance with the Information Release Schedule or mentioned in clause 5 shall be used by the Contractor for any purpose other than this Contract, and neither the Employer, the Architect nor the Quantity Surveyor shall divulge or use except for the purposes of this Contract any of the rates or prices in the Contract Bills.
Issue of Architect's certificates	5·8		Except where otherwise specifically so provided any certificate to be issued by the Architect under the Conditions shall be issued to the Employer, and immediately upon the issue of any such certificate the Architect shall send a duplicate copy thereof to the Contractor.
Supply of as-built drawings etc. – Performance Specified Work	5·9		Before the date of Practical Completion the Contractor shall without further charge to the Employer supply to the Employer such drawings and information showing or describing any Performance Specified Work as built, and concerning the maintenance and operation of any Performance Specified Work including any installations forming a part thereof, as may be specified in the Contract Bills or in an instruction on the expenditure of the provisional sum for the Performance Specified Work.
	6		**Statutory obligations, notices, fees and charges**
Statutory Requirements	6·1	·1	Subject to clause 6·1·5 the Contractor shall comply with, and give all notices required by, any Act of Parliament, any instrument, rule or order made under any Act of Parliament, or any regulation or byelaw of any local authority or of any statutory undertaker which has any jurisdiction with regard to the Works or with whose systems the same are or will be connected (all requirements to be so complied with being referred to in the Conditions as 'the Statutory Requirements').
	6·1	·2	If the Contractor shall find any divergence between the Statutory Requirements and all or any of the documents referred to in clause 2·3 or between the Statutory Requirements and any instruction of the Architect requiring a Variation issued in accordance with clause 13·2, he shall immediately give to the Architect a written notice specifying the divergence.
	6·1	·3	If the Contractor gives notice under clause 6·1·2 or if the Architect shall otherwise discover or receive notice of a divergence between the Statutory Requirements and all or any of the documents referred to in clause 2·3 or between the Statutory Requirements and any instruction requiring a Variation issued in accordance with clause 13·2, the Architect shall within 7 days of the discovery or receipt of a notice issue instructions in relation to the divergence. If and insofar as the instructions require the Works to be varied, they shall be treated as if they were Architect's instructions requiring a Variation issued in accordance with clause 13·2.

6·1 ·4 ·1 If in any emergency compliance with clause 6·1·1 requires the Contractor to supply materials or execute work before receiving instructions under clause 6·1·3 the Contractor shall supply such limited materials and execute such limited work as are reasonably necessary to secure immediate compliance with the Statutory Requirements.

·4 ·2 The Contractor shall forthwith inform the Architect of the emergency and of the steps that he is taking under clause 6·1·4·1.

·4 ·3 Work executed and materials supplied by the Contractor under clause 6·1·4·1 shall be treated as if they had been executed and supplied pursuant to an Architect's instruction requiring a Variation issued in accordance with clause 13·2 provided that the emergency arose because of a divergence between the Statutory Requirements and all or any of the documents referred to in clause 2·3 or between the Statutory Requirements and any instruction requiring a Variation issued in accordance with clause 13·2, and the Contractor has complied with clause 6·1·4·2.

6·1 ·5 Provided that the Contractor complies with clause 6·1·2, the Contractor shall not be liable to the Employer under this Contract if the Works do not comply with the Statutory Requirements where and to the extent that such non-compliance of the Works results from the Contractor having carried out work in accordance with the documents referred to in clause 2·3 or with any instruction requiring a Variation issued by the Architect in accordance with clause 13·2.

Divergence – Statutory Requirements and the Contractor's Statement

6·1 ·6 If the Contractor or the Architect shall find any divergence between the Statutory Requirements and any Contractor's Statement he shall immediately give the other a written notice specifying the divergence. The Contractor shall inform the Architect in writing of his proposed amendment for removing the divergence; and the Architect shall issue instructions in regard thereto. The Contractor's compliance with such instructions shall be subject to clause 42·15 and at no cost to the Employer save as provided in clause 6·1·7.

Change in Statutory Requirements after Base Date

6·1 ·7 If after the Base Date there is a change in the Statutory Requirements which necessitates some alteration or modification to any Performance Specified Work such alteration or modification shall be treated as if it were an instruction of the Architect under clause 13·2 requiring a Variation.

Fees or charges

6·2 The Contractor shall pay and indemnify the Employer against liability in respect of any fees or charges (including any rates or taxes) legally demandable under any Act of Parliament, any instrument, rule or order made under any Act of Parliament, or any regulation or byelaw of any local authority or of any statutory undertaker in respect of the Works. The amount of any such fees or charges (including any rates or taxes other than value added tax) shall be added to the Contract Sum unless they:

6·2 ·1 arise in respect of work executed or materials or goods supplied by a local authority or statutory undertaker as a Nominated Sub-Contractor or as a Nominated Supplier; or

6·2 ·2 are priced in the Contract Bills; or

6·2 ·3 are stated by way of a provisional sum in the Contract Bills.

Exclusion of provisions on Domestic Sub-Contractors and Nominated Sub-Contractors

6·3 The provisions of clauses 19 and 35 shall not apply to the execution of part of the Works by a local authority or a statutory undertaker executing such work solely in pursuance of its statutory obligations and such bodies shall not be sub-contractors within the terms of this Contract.

6A Provisions for use where the Appendix states that all the CDM Regulations apply

Employer's obligation – Planning Supervisor – Principal Contractor

6A·1 The Employer shall ensure:

that the Planning Supervisor carries out all the duties of a planning supervisor under the CDM Regulations; and

where the Contractor is not the Principal Contractor, that the Principal Contractor carries out all the duties of a principal contractor under the CDM Regulations.

Contractor – compliance with duties of a principal contractor

6A·2 Where the Contractor is and while he remains the Principal Contractor, the Contractor shall comply with all the duties of a principal contractor set out in the CDM Regulations; and in particular shall ensure that the Health and Safety Plan has the features required by regulation 15(4) of the CDM Regulations. Any amendment by the Contractor to the Health and Safety Plan shall be notified to the Employer, who shall where relevant thereupon notify the Planning Supervisor and the Architect.

Successor appointed to the Contractor as Principal Contractor

6A·3 Clause 6A·3 applies from the time the Employer pursuant to article 6·2 appoints a successor to the Contractor as the Principal Contractor. The Contractor shall comply at no cost to the Employer with all the reasonable requirements of the Principal Contractor to the extent that such requirements are necessary for compliance with the CDM Regulations; and, notwithstanding clause 25, no extension of time shall be given in respect of such compliance.

Health and safety file

6A·4 Within the time reasonably required in writing by the Planning Supervisor to the Contractor, the Contractor shall provide, and shall ensure that any sub-contractor, through the Contractor, provides, such information to the Planning Supervisor or, if the Contractor is not the Principal Contractor, to the Principal Contractor as the Planning Supervisor reasonably requires for the preparation, pursuant to regulations 14(d), 14(e) and 14(f) of the CDM Regulations, of the health and safety file required by the CDM Regulations.

7 Levels and setting out of the Works

The Architect shall determine any levels which may be required for the execution of the Works, and shall provide the Contractor by way of accurately dimensioned drawings with such information as shall enable the Contractor to set out the Works at ground level. The Contractor shall be responsible for and shall, at no cost to the Employer, amend any errors arising from his own inaccurate setting out. With the consent of the Employer the Architect may instruct that such errors shall not be amended and an appropriate deduction for such errors not required to be amended shall be made from the Contract Sum.

8 Work, materials and goods

Kinds and standards etc.

8·1 ·1 All materials and goods shall, so far as procurable, be of the kinds and standards described in the Contract Bills, and also, in regard to any Performance Specified Work, in the Contractor's Statement, provided that materials and goods shall be to the reasonable satisfaction of the Architect where and to the extent that this is required in accordance with clause 2·1.

8·1 ·2 All workmanship shall be of the standards described in the Contract Bills, and also, in regard to any Performance Specified Work, in the Contractor's Statement, or, to the extent that no such standards are described in the Contract Bills, or, in regard to any Performance Specified Work, in the Contractor's Statement, shall be of a standard appropriate to the Works, provided that workmanship shall be to the reasonable satisfaction of the Architect where and to the extent that this is required in accordance with clause 2·1.

8·1 ·3 All work shall be carried out in a proper and workmanlike manner and in accordance with the Health and Safety Plan.

Construction Skills Certification Scheme

8·1 ·4 The Contractor shall take all reasonable steps to encourage employees and agents of the Contractor and sub-contractors employed in the execution of the Works to be registered cardholders under the Construction Skills Certification Scheme (CSCS) or any successor, or qualified under an equivalent recognised qualification scheme.

Substitution of materials or goods – Performance Specified Work

8·1 ·5 The Contractor shall not substitute any materials or goods described in any Contractor's Statement for Performance Specified Work without the Architect's consent in writing which consent shall not be unreasonably delayed or withheld. No such consent shall relieve the Contractor of any other obligation under this Contract.

Vouchers – materials and goods

8·2 ·1 The Contractor shall upon the request of the Architect provide him with vouchers to prove that the materials and goods comply with clause 8·1.

Executed work	8·2	·2	In respect of any materials, goods or workmanship, as comprised in executed work, which are to be to the reasonable satisfaction of the Architect in accordance with clause 2·1, the Architect shall express any dissatisfaction within a reasonable time from the execution of the unsatisfactory work.
Inspection – tests	8·3		The Architect may issue instructions requiring the Contractor to open up for inspection any work covered up or to arrange for or carry out any test of any materials or goods (whether or not already incorporated in the Works) or of any executed work, and the cost of such opening up or testing (together with the cost of making good in consequence thereof) shall be added to the Contract Sum unless provided for in the Contract Bills or unless the inspection or test shows that the materials, goods or work are not in accordance with this Contract.
Powers of Architect – work not in accordance with the Contract	8·4		If any work, materials or goods are not in accordance with this Contract the Architect, without prejudice to the generality of his powers, may:
	8·4	·1	notwithstanding the power of the Architect under clause 8·4·2, issue instructions in regard to the removal from the site of all or any of such work, materials or goods; and/or
	8·4	·2	after consultation with the Contractor (who shall immediately consult with any relevant Nominated Sub-Contractor) and with the agreement of the Employer, allow all or any of such work, materials or goods to remain and confirm this in writing to the Contractor (which shall not be construed as a Variation) and where so allowed and confirmed an appropriate deduction shall be made in the adjustment of the Contract Sum; and/or
	8·4	·3	after consultation with the Contractor (who shall immediately consult with any relevant Nominated Sub-Contractor) issue such instructions requiring a Variation as are reasonably necessary as a consequence of such an instruction under clause 8·4·1 or such confirmation under clause 8·4·2 and to the extent that such instructions are so necessary and notwithstanding clauses 13·4, 25 and 26 no addition to the Contract Sum shall be made and no extension of time shall be given; and/or
	8·4	·4	having had due regard to the Code of Practice appended to these Conditions *(following clause 42)*, issue such instructions under clause 8·3 to open up for inspection or to test as are reasonable in all the circumstances to establish to the reasonable satisfaction of the Architect the likelihood or extent, as appropriate to the circumstances, of any further similar non-compliance. To the extent that such instructions are so reasonable, whatever the results of the opening up for inspection or test, and notwithstanding clauses 8·3 and 26 no addition to the Contract Sum shall be made. Clause 25·4·5·2 shall apply unless as stated therein the inspection or test showed that the work, materials or goods were not in accordance with this Contract.
Powers of Architect – non-compliance with clause 8·1·3	8·5		Where there is any failure to comply with clause 8·1·3 in regard to the carrying out of the work in a proper and workmanlike manner the Architect, without prejudice to the generality of his powers, may, after consultation with the Contractor (who shall immediately consult with any relevant Nominated Sub-Contractor), issue such instructions whether requiring a Variation or otherwise as are reasonably necessary as a consequence thereof. To the extent that such instructions are so necessary and notwithstanding clauses 13·4 and 25 and 26 no addition to the Contract Sum shall be made and no extension of time shall be given in respect of compliance by the Contractor with such instruction.
Exclusion from the Works of persons employed thereon	8·6		The Architect may (but not unreasonably or vexatiously) issue instructions requiring the exclusion from the site of any person employed thereon.

9 Royalties and patent rights

Treatment of royalties etc. – indemnity to Employer	9·1	All royalties or other sums payable in respect of the supply and use in carrying out the Works as described by or referred to in the Contract Bills of any patented articles, processes or inventions shall be deemed to have been included in the Contract Sum, and the Contractor shall indemnify the Employer from and against all claims, proceedings, damage, costs and expense which may be brought or made against the Employer or to which he may be put by reason of the Contractor infringing or being held to have infringed any patent rights in relation to any such articles, processes or inventions.
Architect's instructions – treatment of royalties etc.	9·2	Provided that where in compliance with Architect's instructions the Contractor shall supply and use in carrying out the Works any patented articles, processes or inventions, the Contractor shall not be liable in respect of any infringement or alleged infringement of any patent rights in relation to any such articles, processes or inventions and all royalties

9·2 *continued*

damages or other monies which the Contractor may be liable to pay to the persons entitled to such patent rights shall be added to the Contract Sum.

10 Person-in-charge

The Contractor shall constantly keep upon the site a competent person-in-charge and any instructions given to him by the Architect or directions given to him by the clerk of works in accordance with clause 12 shall be deemed to have been issued to the Contractor.

11 Access for Architect to the Works

The Architect and his representatives shall at all reasonable times have access to the Works and to the workshops or other places of the Contractor where work is being prepared for this Contract, and when work is to be so prepared in workshops or other places of a Domestic Sub-Contractor or a Nominated Sub-Contractor the Contractor shall by a term in the sub-contract so far as possible secure a similar right of access to those workshops or places for the Architect and his representatives and shall do all things reasonably necessary to make such right effective. Access in accordance with clause 11 may be subject to such reasonable restrictions of the Contractor or any Domestic Sub-Contractor or any Nominated Sub-Contractor as are necessary to protect any proprietary right of the Contractor or of any Domestic or Nominated Sub-Contractor in the work referred to in clause 11.

12 Clerk of works

The Employer shall be entitled to appoint a clerk of works whose duty shall be to act solely as inspector on behalf of the Employer under the directions of the Architect, and the Contractor shall afford every reasonable facility for the performance of that duty. If any direction is given to the Contractor by the clerk of works the same shall be of no effect unless given in regard to a matter in respect of which the Architect is expressly empowered by the Conditions to issue instructions and unless confirmed in writing by the Architect within 2 working days of such direction being given. If any such direction is so given and confirmed then as from the date of issue of that confirmation it shall be deemed to be an Architect's instruction.

13 Variations and provisional sums

Definition of Variation

13·1 The term 'Variation' as used in the Conditions means:

13·1 ·1 the alteration or modification of the design, quality or quantity of the Works including

·1 ·1 the addition, omission or substitution of any work,

·1 ·2 the alteration of the kind or standard of any of the materials or goods to be used in the Works,

·1 ·3 the removal from the site of any work executed or materials or goods brought thereon by the Contractor for the purposes of the Works other than work materials or goods which are not in accordance with this Contract;

13·1 ·2 the imposition by the Employer of any obligations or restrictions in regard to the matters set out in clauses 13·1·2·1 to 13·1·2·4 or the addition to or alteration or omission of any such obligations or restrictions so imposed or imposed by the Employer in the Contract Bills in regard to:

·2 ·1 access to the site or use of any specific parts of the site;

·2 ·2 limitations of working space;

·2 ·3 limitations of working hours;

13·1 ·2 ·4 the execution or completion of the work in any specific order;

but excludes

13·1 ·3 nomination of a sub-contractor to supply and fix materials or goods or to execute work of which the measured quantities have been set out and priced by the Contractor in the Contract Bills for supply and fixing or execution by the Contractor.

Instructions requiring a Variation

13·2 ·1 The Architect may issue instructions requiring a Variation.

13·2 ·2 Any instruction under clause 13·1·2 shall be subject to the Contractor's right of reasonable objection set out in clause 4·1·1.

13·2 ·3 The valuation of a Variation instructed under clause 13·2·1 shall be in accordance with clause 13·4·1·1 unless the instruction states that the treatment and valuation of the Variation are to be in accordance with clause 13A or unless the Variation is one to which clause 13A·8 applies. Where the instruction so states, clause 13A shall apply unless the Contractor within 7 days (or such other period as may be agreed) of receipt of the instruction states in writing that he disagrees with the application of clause 13A to such instruction. If the Contractor so disagrees, clause 13A shall not apply to such instruction and the Variation shall not be carried out unless and until the Architect instructs that the Variation is to be carried out and is to be valued pursuant to clause 13·4·1. [t]

13·2 ·4 The Architect may sanction in writing any Variation made by the Contractor otherwise than pursuant to an instruction of the Architect.

13·2 ·5 No Variation required by the Architect or subsequently sanctioned by him shall vitiate this Contract.

Instructions on provisional sums

13·3 The Architect shall issue instructions in regard to:

13·3 ·1 the expenditure of provisional sums included in the Contract Bills; [u] and

13·3 ·2 the expenditure of provisional sums included in a Nominated Sub-Contract.

Valuation of Variations and provisional sum work and work covered by an Approximate Quantity

13·4 ·1 ·1 Subject to clause 13·4·1·3

– all Variations required by an instruction of the Architect or subsequently sanctioned by him in writing, and

– all work which under the Conditions is to be treated as if it were a Variation required by an instruction of the Architect under clause 13·2, and

– all work executed by the Contractor in accordance with instructions by the Architect as to the expenditure of provisional sums which are included in the Contract Bills, and

– all work executed by the Contractor for which an Approximate Quantity has been included in the Contract Bills

shall, unless otherwise agreed by the Employer and the Contractor, be valued (in the Conditions called 'the Valuation'), under Alternative A in clause 13·4·1·2 or, to the extent that Alternative A is not implemented by the Contractor or, if implemented, to the extent that the Price Statement or amended Price Statement is not accepted, under Alternative B in clause 13·4·1·2. Clause 13·4·1·1 shall not apply in respect of a Variation for which the Architect has issued a confirmed acceptance of a 13A Quotation or is a Variation to which clause 13A·8 applies.

13·4 ·1 ·2 **Alternative A: Contractor's Price Statement**

Paragraph:

A1 Without prejudice to his obligation to comply with any instruction or to execute any work to which clause 13·4·1·1 refers, the Contractor may within 21 days from receipt of the instruction or from commencement of work for which an Approximate Quantity is included in the Contract documents or, if later, from

---

Footnotes

[t] A longer period than 7 days may need to be agreed where the Variation involves a major input from sub-contractors.

[u] If the Architect nominates a sub-contractor or supplier by any instructions under clause 13·3·1, then the provisions of Part 2 of the Conditions apply to such nominations.

13·4 ·1 ·2 A1 *continued*

receipt of sufficient information to enable the Contractor to prepare his Price Statement, submit to the Quantity Surveyor his price ('Price Statement') for such compliance or for such work.

The Price Statement shall state the Contractor's price for the work which shall be based on the provisions of clause 13·5 *(valuation rules)* and may also separately attach the Contractor's requirements for:

- ·1 any amount to be paid in lieu of any ascertainment under clause 26·1 of direct loss and/or expense not included in any accepted 13A Quotation or in any previous ascertainment under clause 26;

- ·2 any adjustment to the time for the completion of the Works to the extent that such adjustment is not included in any revision of the Completion Date that has been made by the Architect under clause 25·3 or in his confirmed acceptance of any 13A Quotation. *(See paragraph A7)*

A2 Within 21 days of receipt of a Price Statement the Quantity Surveyor, after consultation with the Architect, shall notify the Contractor in writing

either

- ·1 that the Price Statement is accepted

or

- ·2 that the Price Statement, or a part thereof, is not accepted.

A3 Where the Price Statement or a part thereof has been accepted the price in that accepted Price Statement or in that part which has been accepted shall in accordance with clause 13·7 be added to or deducted from the Contract Sum.

A4 Where the Price Statement or a part thereof has not been accepted:

- ·1 the Quantity Surveyor shall include in his notification to the Contractor the reasons for not having accepted the Price Statement or a part thereof and set out those reasons in similar detail to that given by the Contractor in his Price Statement and supply an amended Price Statement which is acceptable to the Quantity Surveyor after consultation with the Architect;

- ·2 within 14 days from receipt of the amended Price Statement the Contractor shall state whether or not he accepts the amended Price Statement or part thereof and if accepted paragraph A3 shall apply to that amended Price Statement or part thereof; if no statement within the 14 day period is made the Contractor shall be deemed not to have accepted, in whole or in part, the amended Price Statement;

- ·3 to the extent that the amended Price Statement is not accepted by the Contractor, the Contractor's Price Statement and the amended Price Statement may be referred either by the Employer or by the Contractor as a dispute or difference to the Adjudicator in accordance with the provisions of clause 41A.

A5 Where no notification has been given pursuant to paragraph A2 the Price Statement is deemed not to have been accepted, and the Contractor may, on or after the expiry of the 21 day period to which paragraph A2 refers, refer his Price Statement as a dispute or difference to the Adjudicator in accordance with the provisions of clause 41A.

A6 Where a Price Statement is not accepted by the Quantity Surveyor after consultation with the Architect or an amended Price Statement has not been accepted by the Contractor and no reference to the Adjudicator under paragraph A4·3 or paragraph A5 has been made, Alternative B shall apply.

A7 ·1 Where the Contractor pursuant to paragraph A1 has attached his requirements to his Price Statement the Quantity Surveyor after consultation with the Architect shall within 21 days of receipt thereof notify the Contractor

13·4 ·1 ·2 A7 ·1 ·1 either that the requirement in paragraph A1·1 in respect of the amount to be paid in lieu of any ascertainment under clause 26·1 is accepted or that the requirement is not accepted and clause 26·1 shall apply in respect of the ascertainment of any direct loss and/or expense; and

·1 ·2 either that the requirement in paragraph A1·2 in respect of an adjustment to the time for the completion of the Works is accepted or that the requirement is not accepted and clause 25 shall apply in respect of any such adjustment.

A7 ·2 If the Quantity Surveyor has not notified the Contractor within the 21 days specified in paragraph A7·1, clause 25 and clause 26 shall apply as if no requirements had been attached to the Price Statement.

·1 ·2 **Alternative B**

The Valuation shall be made by the Quantity Surveyor in accordance with the provisions of clauses 13·5·1 to 13·5·7.

·1 ·3 The valuation of Variations to the sub-contract works executed by a Nominated Sub-Contractor in accordance with instructions of the Architect and of all instructions issued under clause 13·3·2 and all work executed by a Nominated Sub-Contractor for which an Approximate Quantity is included in any bills of quantities included in the Numbered Documents shall (unless otherwise agreed by the Contractor and the Nominated Sub-Contractor concerned with the approval of the Employer) be made in accordance with the relevant provisions of Conditions NSC/C.

13·4 ·2 Where under the instruction of the Architect as to the expenditure of a provisional sum a prime cost sum arises and the Contractor under clause 35·2 tenders for the work covered by that prime cost sum and that tender is accepted by or on behalf of the Employer, that work shall be valued in accordance with the accepted tender of the Contractor and shall not be included in the Valuation of the instruction of the Architect in regard to the expenditure of the provisional sum.

Valuation rules **13·5** ·1 To the extent that the Valuation relates to the execution of additional or substituted work which can properly be valued by measurement or to the execution of work for which an Approximate Quantity is included in the Contract Bills such work shall be measured and shall be valued in accordance with the following rules:

·1 ·1 where the additional or substituted work is of similar character to, is executed under similar conditions as, and does not significantly change the quantity of, work set out in the Contract Bills the rates and prices for the work so set out shall determine the Valuation;

·1 ·2 where the additional or substituted work is of similar character to work set out in the Contract Bills but is not executed under similar conditions thereto and/or significantly changes the quantity thereof, the rates and prices for the work so set out shall be the basis for determining the valuation and the valuation shall include a fair allowance for such difference in conditions and/or quantity;

·1 ·3 where the additional or substituted work is not of similar character to work set out in the Contract Bills the work shall be valued at fair rates and prices;

·1 ·4 where the Approximate Quantity is a reasonably accurate forecast of the quantity of work required the rate or price for the Approximate Quantity shall determine the Valuation;

·1 ·5 where the Approximate Quantity is not a reasonably accurate forecast of the quantity of work required the rate or price for that Approximate Quantity shall be the basis for determining the Valuation and the Valuation shall include a fair allowance for such difference in quantity.

Provided that clause 13·5·1·4 and clause 13·5·1·5 shall only apply to the extent that the work has not been altered or modified other than in quantity.

13·5 ·2 To the extent that the Valuation relates to the omission of work set out in the Contract Bills the rates and prices for such work therein set out shall determine the valuation of the work omitted.

13·5 ·3 In any valuation of work under clauses 13·5·1 and 13·5·2:

    ·3 ·1 measurement shall be in accordance with the same principles as those governing the preparation of the Contract Bills as referred to in clause 2·2·2·1;

    ·3 ·2 allowance shall be made for any percentage or lump sum adjustments in the Contract Bills; and

    ·3 ·3 allowance, where appropriate, shall be made for any addition to or reduction of preliminary items of the type referred to in the Standard Method of Measurement; provided that no such allowance shall be made in respect of compliance with an Architect's instruction for the expenditure of a provisional sum for defined work.

13·5 ·4 To the extent that the Valuation relates to the execution of additional or substituted work which cannot properly be valued by measurement the Valuation shall comprise:

    ·4 ·1 the prime cost of such work (calculated in accordance with the 'Definition of Prime Cost of Daywork carried out under a Building Contract' issued by the Royal Institution of Chartered Surveyors and the Building Employers Confederation (now Construction Confederation) which was current at the Base Date) together with percentage additions to each section of the prime cost at the rates set out by the Contractor in the Contract Bills; or

    ·4 ·2 where the work is within the province of any specialist trade and the said Institution and the appropriate [v] body representing the employers in that trade have agreed and issued a definition of prime cost of daywork, the prime cost of such work calculated in accordance with that definition which was current at the Base Date together with percentage additions on the prime cost at the rates set out by the Contractor in the Contract Bills.

    Provided that in any case vouchers specifying the time daily spent upon the work, the workmen's names, the plant and the materials employed shall be delivered for verification to the Architect or his authorised representative not later than the end of the week following that in which the work has been executed.

13·5 ·5 If

    compliance with any instruction requiring a Variation or

    compliance with any instruction as to the expenditure of a provisional sum for undefined work or

    compliance with any instruction as to the expenditure of a provisional sum for defined work to the extent that the instruction for that work differs from the description given for such work in the Contract Bills or

    the execution of work for which an Approximate Quantity is included in the Contract Bills to such extent as the quantity is more or less than the quantity ascribed to that work in the Contract Bills

substantially changes the conditions under which any other work is executed, then such other work shall be treated as if it had been the subject of an instruction of the Architect requiring a Variation under clause 13·2 which shall be valued in accordance with the provisions of clause 13.

13·5 ·6 ·1 The Valuation of Performance Specified Work shall include allowance for the addition or omission of any relevant work involved in the preparation and production of drawings, schedules or other documents;

    ·6 ·2 the Valuation of additional or substituted work related to Performance Specified Work shall be consistent with the rates and prices of work of a similar character set out in the Contract Bills or the Analysis making due allowance for any changes in the conditions under which the work is carried out and/or any significant change in the quantity of the work set out in the Contract Bills or in the Contractor's Statement. Where there is no work of a similar character set out in the Contract Bills or the Contractor's Statement a fair valuation shall be made;

Footnote   [v] There are three Definitions to which clause 13·5·4·2 refers namely those agreed between the Royal Institution and the Electrical Contractors Association, the Royal Institution and the Electrical Contractors Association of Scotland and the Royal Institution and the Heating and Ventilating Contractors Association.

13·5 *continued*

·6 ·3 the Valuation of the omission of work relating to Performance Specified Work shall be in accordance with the rates and prices for such work set out in the Contract Bills or the Analysis;

·6 ·4 any valuation of work under clauses 13·5·6·2 and 13·5·6·3 shall include allowance for any necessary addition to or reduction of preliminary items of the type referred to in the Standard Method of Measurement;

·6 ·5 where an appropriate basis of a fair valuation of additional or substituted work relating to Performance Specified Work is daywork the Valuation shall be in accordance with clauses 13·5·4·1 or 13·5·4·2 and the proviso to clause 13·5·4 shall apply;

·6 ·6 if

compliance with any instruction under clause 42·11 requiring a Variation to Performance Specified Work or

compliance with any instruction as to the expenditure of a provisional sum for Performance Specified Work to the extent that the instruction for that Work differs from the information provided in the Contract Bills pursuant to clause 42·7·2 and/or 42·7·3 for such Performance Specified Work

substantially changes the conditions under which any other work is executed (including any other Performance Specified Work) then such other work (including any other Performance Specified Work) shall be treated as if it had been the subject of an instruction of the Architect requiring a Variation under clause 13·2 or, if relevant, under clause 42·11 which shall be valued in accordance with the provisions of clause 13·5.

13·5 ·7 To the extent that the Valuation does not relate to the execution of additional or substituted work or the omission of work or to the extent that the valuation of any work or liabilities directly associated with a Variation cannot reasonably be effected in the Valuation by the application of clauses 13·5·1 to ·6 a fair valuation thereof shall be made.

Provided that no allowance shall be made under clause 13·5 for any effect upon the regular progress of the Works or for any other direct loss and/or expense for which the Contractor would be reimbursed by payment under any other provision in the Conditions.

Contractor's right to be present at measurement

13·6 Where it is necessary to measure work for the purpose of the Valuation the Quantity Surveyor shall give to the Contractor an opportunity of being present at the time of such measurement and of taking such notes and measurements as the Contractor may require.

Valuations – Employer/Contractor agreement – 13A Quotation for a Variation and Variations thereto – addition to or deduction from Contract Sum

13·7 Effect shall be given to the Valuation under clause 13·4·1·1, to an agreement by the Employer and the Contractor to which clause 13·4·1·1 refers, to a 13A Quotation for which the Architect has issued a confirmed acceptance and to a valuation pursuant to clause 13A·8 by addition to or deduction from the Contract Sum.

13A Variation instruction – Contractor's quotation in compliance with the instruction

Contractor to submit his quotation ('13A Quotation')

13A Clause 13A shall only apply to an instruction where pursuant to clause 13·2·3 the Contractor has not disagreed with the application of clause 13A to such instruction.

13A·1 ·1 The instruction to which clause 13A is to apply shall have provided sufficient information [w] to enable the Contractor to provide a quotation, which shall comprise the matters set out in clause 13A·2 (a '13A Quotation'), in compliance with the instruction; and in respect of any part of the Variation which relates to the work of any Nominated Sub-Contractor sufficient information to enable the Contractor to obtain a 3·3A Quotation from the Nominated Sub-Contractor in accordance with clause 3·3A·1·2 of the Conditions NSC/C. If the Contractor reasonably considers that the information provided is not sufficient, then, not later than 7 days from the receipt of the instruction, he shall request the Architect to supply sufficient further information.

Footnote

[w] The information provided to the Contractor should normally be in a similar format to that provided at the tender stage; and may be in the form of drawings and/or in an addendum bill of quantities and/or in a specification or otherwise. If an addendum bill is provided see the relevant provisions in clause 2·2·2.

13A·1 ·2 The Contractor shall submit to the Quantity Surveyor his 13A Quotation in compliance with the instruction and shall include therein 3·3A Quotations in respect of any parts of the Variation which relate to the work of Nominated Sub-Contractors not later than 21 days from

> the date of receipt of the instruction

> or if applicable, the date of receipt by the Contractor of the sufficient further information to which clause 13A·1·1 refers

whichever date is the later and the 13A Quotation shall remain open for acceptance by the Employer for 7 days from its receipt by the Quantity Surveyor.

13A·1 ·3 The Variation for which the Contractor has submitted his 13A Quotation shall not be carried out by the Contractor or as relevant by any Nominated Sub-Contractor until receipt by the Contractor of the confirmed acceptance issued by the Architect pursuant to clause 13A·3·2.

Content of the Contractor's 13A Quotation

13A·2 The 13A Quotation shall separately comprise:

13A·2 ·1 the value of the adjustment to the Contract Sum (other than any amount to which clause 13A·2·3 refers) including therein the effect of the instruction on any other work including that of Nominated Sub-Contractors supported by all necessary calculations by reference, where relevant, to the rates and prices in the Contract Bills and including, where appropriate, allowances for any adjustment of preliminary items;

13A·2 ·2 any adjustment to the time required for completion of the Works (including where relevant stating an earlier Completion Date than the Date for Completion given in the Appendix) to the extent that such adjustment is not included in any revision of the Completion Date that has been made by the Architect under clause 25·3 or in his confirmed acceptance of any other 13A Quotation;

13A·2 ·3 the amount to be paid in lieu of any ascertainment under clause 26·1 of direct loss and/or expense not included in any other accepted 13A Quotation or in any previous ascertainment under clause 26;

13A·2 ·4 a fair and reasonable amount in respect of the cost of preparing the 13A Quotation;

and, where specifically required by the instruction, shall provide indicative information in statements on

13A·2 ·5 the additional resources (if any) required to carry out the Variation; and

13A·2 ·6 the method of carrying out the Variation.

Each part of the 13A Quotation shall contain reasonably sufficient supporting information to enable that part to be evaluated by or on behalf of the Employer.

Acceptance of 13A Quotation – Architect's confirmed acceptance

13A·3 ·1 If the Employer wishes to accept a 13A Quotation the Employer shall so notify the Contractor in writing not later than the last day of the period for acceptance stated in clause 13A·1·2.

13A·3 ·2 If the Employer accepts a 13A Quotation the Architect shall, immediately upon that acceptance, confirm such acceptance by stating in writing to the Contractor (in clause 13A and elsewhere in the Conditions called a 'confirmed acceptance'):

·2 ·1 that the Contractor is to carry out the Variation;

·2 ·2 the adjustment of the Contract Sum, including therein any amounts to which clause 13A·2·3 and clause 13A·2·4 refer, to be made for complying with the instruction requiring the Variation;

·2 ·3 any adjustment to the time required by the Contractor for completion of the Works and the revised Completion Date arising therefrom (which, where relevant, may be a date earlier than the Date for Completion given in the Appendix) and, where relevant, any revised period or periods for the completion of the Nominated Sub-Contract work of each Nominated Sub-Contractor; and

13A·3 *continued*

·2 ·4 that the Contractor, pursuant to clause 3·3A·3 of the Conditions NSC/C, shall accept any 3·3A Quotation included in the 13A Quotation for which the confirmed acceptance has been issued.

Contractor's 13A Quotation not accepted

13A·4 If the Employer does not accept the 13A Quotation by the expiry of the period for acceptance stated in clause 13A·1·2, the Architect shall, on the expiry of that period,

either

13A·4 ·1 instruct that the Variation is to be carried out and is to be valued pursuant to clause 13·4·1;

or

13A·4 ·2 instruct that the Variation is not to be carried out.

Payment for a 13A Quotation

13A·5 If a 13A Quotation is not accepted a fair and reasonable amount shall be added to the Contract Sum in respect of the cost of preparation of the 13A Quotation provided that the 13A Quotation has been prepared on a fair and reasonable basis. The non-acceptance by the Employer of a 13A Quotation shall not of itself be evidence that the Quotation was not prepared on a fair and reasonable basis.

Restriction on use of a 13A Quotation

13A·6 If the Architect has not, under clause 13A·3·2, issued a confirmed acceptance of a 13A Quotation neither the Employer nor the Contractor may use that 13A Quotation for any purpose whatsoever.

Number of days – clauses 13A·1·1 and/or 13A·1·2

13A·7 The Employer and the Contractor may agree to increase or reduce the number of days stated in clause 13A·1·1 and/or in clause 13A·1·2 and any such agreement shall be confirmed in writing by the Employer to the Contractor. Where relevant the Contractor shall notify each Nominated Sub-Contractor of any agreed increase or reduction pursuant to this clause 13A·7.

Variations to work for which a confirmed acceptance of a 13A Quotation has been issued – valuation

13A·8 If the Architect issues an instruction requiring a Variation to work for which a 13A Quotation has been given and in respect of which the Architect has issued a confirmed acceptance to the Contractor such Variation shall not be valued under clause 13·5; but the Quantity Surveyor shall make a valuation of such Variation on a fair and reasonable basis having regard to the content of such 13A Quotation and shall include in that valuation the direct loss and/or expense, if any, incurred by the Contractor because the regular progress of the Works or any part thereof has been materially affected by compliance with the instruction requiring the Variation.

14 Contract Sum

Quality and quantity of work included in Contract Sum

14·1 The quality and quantity of the work included in the Contract Sum shall be deemed to be that which is set out in the Contract Bills.

Contract Sum – only adjusted under the Conditions – errors in computation

14·2 The Contract Sum shall not be adjusted or altered in any way whatsoever otherwise than in accordance with the express provisions of the Conditions, and subject to clause 2·2·2·2 any error whether of arithmetic or not in the computation of the Contract Sum shall be deemed to have been accepted by the parties hereto.

15 Value added tax – supplemental provisions

Definitions – VAT Agreement

15·1 In clause 15 and in the supplemental provisions pursuant hereto (hereinafter called the 'VAT Agreement') 'tax' means the value added tax introduced by the Finance Act 1972 which is under the care and management of the Commissioners of Customs and Excise (hereinafter and in the VAT Agreement called 'the Commissioners').

Contract Sum – exclusive of VAT	15·2	Any reference in the Conditions to 'Contract Sum' shall be regarded as such Sum exclusive of any tax and recovery by the Contractor from the Employer of tax properly chargeable by the Commissioners on the Contractor under or by virtue of the Value Added Tax Act 1994 or any amendment or re-enactment thereof on the supply of goods and services under this Contract shall be under the provisions of clause 15 and of the VAT Agreement. Clause 1A of the VAT Agreement shall only apply where so stated in the Appendix. [x]
Possible exemption from VAT	15·3	To the extent that after the Base Date the supply of goods and services to the Employer becomes exempt from the tax there shall be paid to the Contractor an amount equal to the loss of credit (input tax) on the supply to the Contractor of goods and services which contribute exclusively to the Works.

16 Materials and goods unfixed or off-site

Unfixed materials and goods – on site	16·1	Unfixed materials and goods delivered to, placed on or adjacent to the Works and intended therefor shall not be removed except for use upon the Works unless the Architect has consented in writing to such removal which consent shall not be unreasonably delayed or withheld. Where the value of any such materials or goods has in accordance with clause 30·2 been included in any Interim Certificate under which the amount properly due to the Contractor has been paid by the Employer, such materials and goods shall become the property of the Employer, but, subject to clause 22B or 22C (if applicable), the Contractor shall remain responsible for loss or damage to the same.
Unfixed materials and goods – off-site	16·2	Where the value of any 'listed items' has in accordance with clause 30·3 been included in any Interim Certificate under which the amount properly due to the Contractor has been paid by the Employer, such listed items shall become the property of the Employer and thereafter the Contractor shall not, except for use upon the Works, remove or cause or permit the same to be moved or removed from the premises where they are, but the Contractor shall nevertheless be responsible for any loss thereof or damage thereto and for the cost of storage, handling and insurance of the same until such time as they are delivered to and placed on or adjacent to the Works whereupon the provisions of clause 16·1 (except the words "Where the value" to the words "the property of the Employer, but,") shall apply thereto.

17 Practical Completion and defects liability

Certificate of Practical Completion	17·1	When in the opinion of the Architect Practical Completion of the Works is achieved and the Contractor has complied sufficiently with clause 6A·4, and, if relevant, the Contractor has complied with clause 5·9 *(Supply of as-built drawings etc. – Performance Specified Work)*, he shall forthwith issue a certificate to that effect and Practical Completion of the Works shall be deemed for all the purposes of this Contract to have taken place on the day named in such certificate.
Defects, shrinkages or other faults	17·2	Any defects, shrinkages or other faults which shall appear within the Defects Liability Period and which are due to materials or workmanship not in accordance with this Contract or to frost occurring before Practical Completion of the Works, shall be specified by the Architect in a schedule of defects which he shall deliver to the Contractor as an instruction of the Architect not later than 14 days after the expiration of the said Defects Liability Period, and within a reasonable time after receipt of such schedule the defects, shrinkages and other faults therein specified shall be made good by the Contractor at no cost to the Employer unless the Architect with the consent of the Employer shall otherwise instruct; and if the Architect does so otherwise instruct then an appropriate deduction in respect of any such defects, shrinkages or other faults not made good shall be made from the Contract Sum.
Defects etc. – Architect's instructions	17·3	Notwithstanding clause 17·2 the Architect may whenever he considers it necessary so to do issue instructions requiring any defect, shrinkage or other fault which shall appear within the Defects Liability Period and which is due to materials or workmanship not in accordance with this Contract or to frost occurring before Practical Completion of the Works, to be made good, and the Contractor shall within a reasonable time after receipt of such instructions comply with the same at no cost to the Employer unless the Architect with the consent of the

---

Footnote [x] Clause 1A can only apply where the Contractor is satisfied at the date the Contract is entered into that his output tax on **all** supplies to the Employer under the Contract will be at either a positive or a zero rate of tax.

17·3 *continued*

Employer shall otherwise instruct; and if the Architect does so otherwise instruct then an appropriate deduction in respect of any such defects, shrinkages or other faults not made good shall be made from the Contract Sum. Provided that no such instructions shall be issued after delivery of a schedule of defects or after 14 days from the expiration of the Defects Liability Period.

Certificate of Completion of Making Good Defects

17·4 When in the opinion of the Architect any defects, shrinkages or other faults which he may have required to be made good under clauses 17·2 and 17·3 shall have been made good he shall issue a certificate to that effect, and completion of making good defects shall be deemed for all the purposes of this Contract to have taken place on the day named in such certificate (the 'Certificate of Completion of Making Good Defects').

Damage by frost

17·5 In no case shall the Contractor be required to make good at his own cost any damage by frost which may appear after Practical Completion, unless the Architect shall certify that such damage is due to injury which took place before Practical Completion.

18 Partial possession by Employer

Employer's wish – Contractor's consent

18·1 If at any time or times before the date of issue by the Architect of the certificate of Practical Completion the Employer wishes to take possession of any part or parts of the Works and the consent of the Contractor (which consent shall not be unreasonably delayed or withheld) has been obtained, then, notwithstanding anything expressed or implied elsewhere in this Contract, the Employer may take possession thereof. The Architect shall thereupon issue to the Contractor on behalf of the Employer a written statement identifying the part or parts of the Works taken into possession and giving the date when the Employer took possession (in clauses 18, 20·3, 22·3·1 and 22C·1 referred to as 'the relevant part' and 'the relevant date' respectively).

Practical Completion – relevant part

18·1 ·1 For the purposes of clauses 17·2, 17·3, 17·5 and 30·4·1·2 Practical Completion of the relevant part shall be deemed to have occurred and the Defects Liability Period in respect of the relevant part shall be deemed to have commenced on the relevant date.

Defects etc. – relevant part

18·1 ·2 When in the opinion of the Architect any defects, shrinkages or other faults in the relevant part which he may have required to be made good under clause 17·2 or clause 17·3 shall have been made good he shall issue a certificate to that effect.

Insurance – relevant part

18·1 ·3 As from the relevant date the obligation of the Contractor under clause 22A or of the Employer under clause 22B·1 or clause 22C·2 whichever is applicable to insure shall terminate in respect of the relevant part but not further or otherwise; and where clause 22C applies the obligation of the Employer to insure under clause 22C·1 shall from the relevant date include the relevant part.

Liquidated damages – relevant part

18·1 ·4 In lieu of any sum to be paid by the Contractor or withheld or deducted by the Employer under clause 24 in respect of any period during which the Works may remain incomplete occurring after the relevant date there shall be paid such sum as bears the same ratio to the sum which would be paid apart from the provisions of clause 18 as the Contract Sum less the amount contained therein in respect of the relevant part bears to the Contract Sum; or the Employer may give a notice pursuant to clause 30·1·1·4 that he will deduct such sum from the monies due to the Contractor.

19 Assignment and sub-contracts

Assignment

19·1 ·1 Neither the Employer nor the Contractor shall, without the written consent of the other, assign this Contract.

19·1 ·2 Where clause 19·1·2 is stated in the Appendix to apply then, in the event of transfer by the Employer of his freehold or leasehold interest in, or of a grant by the Employer of a leasehold interest in, the whole of the premises comprising the Works, the Employer may at any time after Practical Completion of the Works assign to any such transferee or lessee the right to bring proceedings in the name of the Employer (whether by arbitration or litigation) to enforce any of the terms of this Contract made for the benefit of the Employer hereunder. The assignee shall be estopped from disputing any enforceable agreements reached between the Employer and the Contractor and which

19·1 ·2 *continued*

arise out of and relate to this Contract (whether or not they are or appear to be a derogation from the right assigned) and made prior to the date of any assignment.

Sub-letting – Domestic Sub-Contractors – Architect's consent

19·2 ·1 A person to whom the Contractor sub-lets any portion of the Works other than a Nominated Sub-Contractor is in this Contract referred to as a 'Domestic Sub-Contractor'.

19·2 ·2 The Contractor shall not without the written consent of the Architect (which consent shall not be unreasonably delayed or withheld) sub-let any portion of the Works. The Contractor shall remain wholly responsible for carrying out and completing the Works in all respects in accordance with clause 2·1 notwithstanding the sub-letting of any portion of the Works.

Sub-letting – list in Contract Bills

19·3 ·1 Where the Contract Bills provide that certain work measured or otherwise described in those Bills and priced by the Contractor must be carried out by persons named in a list in or annexed to the Contract Bills and selected therefrom by and at the sole discretion of the Contractor the provisions of clause 19·3 shall apply in respect of that list.

19·3 ·2 ·1 The list referred to in clause 19·3·1 must comprise not less than three persons. Either the Employer (or the Architect on his behalf) or the Contractor shall be entitled with the consent of the other, which consent shall not be unreasonably delayed or withheld, to add [y] additional persons to the list at any time prior to the execution of a binding sub-contract agreement.

·2 ·2 If at any time prior to the execution of a binding sub-contract agreement and for whatever reason less than three persons named in the list are able and willing to carry out the relevant work then

either the Employer and the Contractor shall by agreement (which agreement shall not be unreasonably delayed or withheld) add [y] the names of other persons so that the list comprises not less than three such persons

or the work shall be carried out by the Contractor who may sub-let to a Domestic Sub-Contractor in accordance with clause 19·2.

19·3 ·3 A person selected by the Contractor under clause 19·3 from the aforesaid list shall be a Domestic Sub-Contractor.

Sub-letting – conditions of any sub-letting

19·4 It shall be a condition in any sub-letting to which clause 19·2 or 19·3 refers that:

19·4 ·1 the employment of the Domestic Sub-Contractor under the sub-contract shall determine immediately upon the determination (for any reason) of the Contractor's employment under this Contract; and

19·4 ·2 the sub-contract shall provide that:

·2 ·1 subject to clause 16·1 of these Conditions (in clauses 19·4·2·2 to ·4 called 'the Main Contract Conditions'), unfixed materials and goods delivered to, placed on or adjacent to the Works by the sub-contractor and intended therefor shall not be removed except for use on the Works unless the Contractor has consented in writing to such removal, which consent shall not be unreasonably delayed or withheld;

·2 ·2 where, in accordance with clause 30·2 of the Main Contract Conditions, the value of any such materials or goods shall have been included in any Interim Certificate under which the amount properly due to the Contractor shall have been paid by the Employer to the Contractor, such materials or goods shall be and become the property of the Employer and the sub-contractor shall not deny that such materials or goods are and have become the property of the Employer;

Footnote [y] Any such addition must be initialled by or on behalf of the Parties.

19·4 *continued*

·2 ·3 provided that if the Contractor shall pay the sub-contractor for any such materials or goods before the value therefor has, in accordance with clause 30·2 of the Main Contract Conditions, been included in any Interim Certificate under which the amount properly due to the Contractor has been paid by the Employer to the Contractor, such materials or goods shall upon such payment by the Contractor be and become the property of the Contractor;

·2 ·4 the operation of clauses 19·4·2·1 to ·3 hereof shall be without prejudice to any property in any materials or goods passing to the Contractor as provided in clause 30·3 of the Main Contract Conditions *(off-site materials or goods)*; and

19·4 ·3 the sub-contract shall provide that if the Contractor fails properly to pay the amount, or any part thereof, due to the sub-contractor by the final date for its payment stated in the sub-contract, the Contractor shall pay to the sub-contractor in addition to the amount not properly paid simple interest thereon for the period until such payment is made; that the payment of such simple interest shall be treated as a debt due to the sub-contractor by the Contractor; that the rate of interest payable shall be five per cent (5%) over the Base Rate of the Bank of England which is current at the date the payment by the Contractor became overdue; and that any payment of simple interest shall not in any circumstances be construed as a waiver by the sub-contractor of his right to proper payment of the principal amounts due from the Contractor to the sub-contractor in accordance with, and within the time stated in, the sub-contract or of any rights of the sub-contractor under the sub-contract in regard to suspension of the performance of his obligations to the Contractor under the sub-contract or determination of his employment for the failure by the Contractor properly to pay any amount due under the sub-contract to the sub-contractor.

Nominated Sub-Contractors

19·5 ·1 The provisions of this Contract relating to Nominated Sub-Contractors are set out in Part 2 of the Conditions. Save as otherwise expressed in the Conditions the Contractor shall remain wholly responsible for carrying out and completing the Works in all respects in accordance with clause 2·1, notwithstanding the nomination of a sub-contractor to supply and fix materials or goods or to execute work.

19·5 ·2 Subject to clause 35·2 the Contractor is not himself required, unless otherwise agreed, to supply and fix materials or goods or to execute work which is to be carried out by a Nominated Sub-Contractor.

20 Injury to persons and property and indemnity to Employer

Liability of Contractor – personal injury or death – indemnity to Employer

20·1 The Contractor shall be liable for, and shall indemnify the Employer against, any expense, liability, loss, claim or proceedings whatsoever arising under any statute or at common law in respect of personal injury to or the death of any person whomsoever arising out of or in the course of or caused by the carrying out of the Works, except to the extent that the same is due to any act or neglect of the Employer or of any person for whom the Employer is responsible including the persons employed or otherwise engaged by the Employer to whom clause 29 refers.

Liability of Contractor – injury or damage to property – indemnity to Employer

20·2 The Contractor shall be liable for, and shall indemnify the Employer against, any expense, liability, loss, claim or proceedings in respect of any loss, injury or damage whatsoever to any property real or personal in so far as such loss, injury or damage arises out of or in the course of or by reason of the carrying out of the Works and to the extent that the same is due to any negligence, breach of statutory duty, omission or default of the Contractor, his servants or agents or of any person employed or engaged upon or in connection with the Works or any part thereof, his servants or agents or of any other person who may properly be on the site upon or in connection with the Works or any part thereof, his servants or agents, other than the Employer or any person employed, engaged or authorised by him or by any local authority or statutory undertaker executing work solely in pursuance of its statutory rights or obligations. This liability and indemnity is subject to clause 20·3 and, where clause 22C·1 is applicable, excludes loss or damage to any property required to be insured thereunder caused by a Specified Peril.

Injury or damage to property – exclusion of the Works and Site Materials

20·3 ·1 Subject to clause 20·3·2 the reference in clause 20·2 to 'property real or personal' does not include the Works, work executed and/or Site Materials up to and including the date of issue of the certificate of Practical Completion or up to and including the date of determination of the employment of the Contractor (whether or not the validity of that determination is disputed) under clause 27 or clause 28 or clause 28A or, where clause 22C applies, under clause 27 or clause 28 or clause 28A or clause 22C·4·3, whichever is the earlier.

20·3 ·2 If clause 18 has been operated then, in respect of the relevant part and as from the relevant date, such relevant part shall not be regarded as 'the Works' or 'work executed' for the purpose of clause 20·3·1.

21 Insurance against injury to persons or property

Contractor's insurance – personal injury or death – injury or damage to property

21·1 ·1 ·1 Without prejudice to his obligation to indemnify the Employer under clause 20 the Contractor shall take out and maintain insurance which shall comply with clause 21·1·1·2 in respect of claims arising out of his liability referred to in clauses 20·1 and 20·2.

·1 ·2 The insurance in respect of claims for personal injury to or the death of any person under a contract of service or apprenticeship with the Contractor, and arising out of and in the course of such person's employment, shall comply with all relevant legislation. For all other claims to which clause 21·1·1·1 applies the insurance cover [z]:

– shall indemnify the Employer in like manner to the Contractor but only to the extent that the Contractor may be liable to indemnify the Employer under the terms of this Contract; and

– shall be not less than the sum stated in the Appendix [aa] for any one occurrence or series of occurrences arising out of one event.

21·1 ·2 As and when he is reasonably required to do so by the Employer the Contractor shall send to the Architect for inspection by the Employer documentary evidence that the insurances required by clause 21·1·1·1 have been taken out and are being maintained, but at any time the Employer may (but not unreasonably or vexatiously) require to have sent to the Architect for inspection by the Employer the relevant policy or policies and the premium receipts therefor.

21·1 ·3 If the Contractor defaults in taking out or in maintaining insurance as provided in clause 21·1·1·1 the Employer may himself insure against any liability or expense which he may incur arising out of such default and a sum or sums equivalent to the amount paid or payable by him in respect of premiums therefor may be deducted by him from any monies due or to become due to the Contractor under this Contract or such amount may be recoverable by the Employer from the Contractor as a debt.

Insurance – liability etc. of Employer

21·2 ·1 Where it is stated in the Appendix that the insurance to which clause 21·2·1 refers may be required by the Employer the Contractor shall, if so instructed by the Architect, take out a policy of insurance in the names of the Employer and the Contractor [bb] for such amount of indemnity as is stated in the Appendix in respect of any expense, liability, loss, claim or proceedings which the Employer may incur or sustain by reason of injury or damage to any property caused by collapse, subsidence, heave, vibration, weakening or removal of support or lowering of ground water arising out of or in the course of or by reason of the carrying out of the Works excepting injury or damage:

·1 ·1 for which the Contractor is liable under clause 20·2;

·1 ·2 attributable to errors or omissions in the designing of the Works;

·1 ·3 which can reasonably be foreseen to be inevitable having regard to the nature of the work to be executed and the manner of its execution;

Footnotes

[z] It should be noted that the cover granted under public liability policies taken out pursuant to clause 21·1·1 may not be co-extensive with the indemnity given to the Employer in clauses 20·1 and 20·2: for example each claim may be subject to the excess in the policy and cover may not be available in respect of loss or damage due to gradual pollution.

[aa] The Contractor may, if he so wishes, insure for a sum greater than that stated in the Appendix.

[bb] A policy of insurance taken out for the purposes of clause 21·2 should not have an expiry date earlier than the end of the Defects Liability Period.

21·2 *continued*

·1 ·4 which it is the responsibility of the Employer to insure under clause 22C·1 (if applicable);

·1 ·5 to the Works and Site Materials brought on to the site of the Contract for the purpose of its execution except in so far as any part or parts thereof are the subject of a certificate of Practical Completion;

·1 ·6 arising from any consequence of war, invasion, act of foreign enemy, hostilities (whether war be declared or not), civil war, rebellion or revolution, insurrection or military or usurped power;

·1 ·7 directly or indirectly caused by or contributed to by or arising from the Excepted Risks;

·1 ·8 directly or indirectly caused by or arising out of pollution or contamination of buildings or other structure or of water or land or the atmosphere happening during the period of insurance; save that this exception shall not apply in respect of pollution or contamination caused by a sudden identifiable, unintended and unexpected incident which takes place in its entirety at a specific moment in time and place during the period of insurance provided that all pollution or contamination which arises out of one incident shall be considered for the purpose of this insurance to have occurred at the time such incident takes place;

·1 ·9 which results in any costs or expenses being incurred by the Employer or in any other sums being payable by the Employer in respect of damages for breach of contract except to the extent that such costs or expenses or damages would have attached in the absence of any contract.

21·2 ·2 Any such insurance as is referred to in clause 21·2·1 shall be placed with insurers to be approved by the Employer, and the Contractor shall send to the Architect for deposit with the Employer the policy or policies and the premium receipts therefor.

21·2 ·3 The amounts expended by the Contractor to take out and maintain the insurance referred to in clause 21·2·1 shall be added to the Contract Sum.

21·2 ·4 If the Contractor defaults in taking out or in maintaining the Joint Names Policy as provided in clause 21·2·1 the Employer may himself insure against any risk in respect of which the default shall have occurred.

Excepted Risks 21·3 Notwithstanding the provisions of clauses 20·1, 20·2 and 21·1·1, the Contractor shall not be liable either to indemnify the Employer or to insure against any personal injury to or the death of any person or any damage, loss or injury caused to the Works or Site Materials, work executed, the site, or any property, by the effect of an Excepted Risk.

22 Insurance of the Works [cc]

Insurance of the Works – alternative clauses
22·1 Clause 22A or clause 22B or clause 22C shall apply whichever clause is stated to apply in the Appendix.

Footnote

[cc] **Clause 22A** is applicable to the erection of new buildings where the **Contractor** is required to take out a Joint Names Policy for All Risks Insurance for the Works and **clause 22B** is applicable where the **Employer** has elected to take out such Joint Names Policy. **Clause 22C** is to be used for alterations of or extensions to existing structures under which the **Employer** is required to take out a Joint Names Policy for All Risks Insurance for the Works and also a Joint Names Policy to insure the existing structures and their contents owned by him or for which he is responsible against loss or damage thereto by the Specified Perils.

Definitions **22·2** In clauses 22A, 22B, 22C and, so far as relevant, in other clauses of the Conditions the following phrases shall have the meanings given below:

All Risks Insurance: [dd]   insurance which provides cover against any physical loss or damage to work executed and Site Materials and against the reasonable cost of the removal and disposal of debris and of any shoring and propping of the Works which results from such physical loss or damage but excluding the cost necessary to repair, replace or rectify

1   property which is defective due to

·1   wear and tear,

·2   obsolescence,

·3   deterioration, rust or mildew;

[ee] 2   any work executed or any Site Materials lost or damaged as a result of its own defect in design, plan, specification, material or workmanship or any other work executed which is lost or damaged in consequence thereof where such work relied for its support or stability on such work which was defective;

3   loss or damage caused by or arising from

·1   any consequence of war, invasion, act of foreign enemy, hostilities (whether war be declared or not), civil war, rebellion, revolution, insurrection, military or usurped power, confiscation, commandeering, nationalisation or requisition or loss or destruction of or damage to any property by or under the order of any government *de jure* or *de facto* or public, municipal or local authority;

·2   disappearance or shortage if such disappearance or shortage is only revealed when an inventory is made or is not traceable to an identifiable event;

·3   an Excepted Risk (as defined in clause 1·3).

Joint Names Policy: a policy of insurance which includes the Employer and the Contractor as the insured and under which the insurers have no right of recourse against any person named as an insured, or, pursuant to clause 22·3, recognised as an insured thereunder.

terrorism: any act of any person acting on behalf of or in connection with any organisation with activities directed towards the overthrowing or influencing of any government *de jure* or *de facto* by force or violence.

terrorism cover: insurance provided under a Joint Names Policy to which clauses 22A, 22B and 22C refer for physical loss or damage to work executed and Site Materials and to an existing structure and/or its contents due to fire or explosion caused by terrorism.

Footnotes

[dd] The definition of 'All Risks Insurance' in clause 22·2 defines the risks for which insurance is required. Policies issued by insurers are not standardised and there will be some variation in the way the insurance for those risks is expressed. See also Practice Note 22 and Guide, Part A.

[ee] In any policy for 'All Risks Insurance' taken out under clauses 22A, 22B or 22C·2 cover should not be reduced by the terms of any exclusion written in the policy beyond the terms of paragraph 2; thus an exclusion in terms "This Policy excludes all loss of or damage to the property insured due to defective design, plan, specification, materials or workmanship" would not be in accordance with the terms of those clauses and of the definition of 'All Risks Insurance'. Cover which goes beyond the terms of the exclusion in paragraph 2 may be available though not standard in all policies taken out to meet the obligation in clauses 22A, 22B or 22C·2: and leading insurers who underwrite 'All Risks' cover for the Works have confirmed that where such improved cover is being given it will not be withdrawn as a consequence of the publication of the terms of the definition in clause 22·2 of 'All Risks Insurance'.

Nominated and Domestic Sub-Contractors – benefit of Joint Names Policies – Specified Perils

22·3 ·1 The Contractor where clause 22A applies, and the Employer where either clause 22B or clause 22C applies, shall ensure that the Joint Names Policy referred to in clause 22A·1 or clause 22A·3 or the Joint Names Policies referred to in clause 22B·1 or in clauses 22C·1 and 22C·2 shall

either provide for recognition of each sub-contractor nominated by the Architect as an insured under the relevant Joint Names Policy

or include a waiver by the relevant insurers of any right of subrogation which they may have against any such Nominated Sub-Contractor

in respect of loss or damage by the Specified Perils to the Works and Site Materials where clause 22A or clause 22B or clause 22C·2 applies and, where clause 22C·1 applies, in respect of loss or damage by the Specified Perils to the existing structures (which shall include from the relevant date any relevant part to which clause 18·1·3 refers) together with the contents thereof owned by the Employer or for which he is responsible; and that this recognition or waiver shall continue up to and including the date of issue of the certificate of practical completion of the sub-contract works (as referred to in clause 2·11 of Conditions NSC/C) or the date of determination of the employment of the Contractor (whether or not the validity of that determination is contested) under clause 27 or clause 28 or clause 28A or, where 22C applies, under clause 27 or clause 28 or clause 28A or clause 22C·4·3, whichever is the earlier. The provisions of clause 22·3·1 shall apply also in respect of any Joint Names Policy taken out by the Employer under clause 22A·2 or by the Contractor under clause 22B·2 or under clause 22C·3 in respect of a default by the Employer under clause 22C·2.

22·3 ·2 Except in respect of the Joint Names Policy referred to in clause 22C·1 (or the Joint Names Policy referred to in clause 22C·3 in respect of a default by the Employer under clause 22C·1) the provisions of clause 22·3·1 in regard to recognition or waiver shall apply to Domestic Sub-Contractors. Such recognition or waiver for Domestic Sub-Contractors shall continue up to and including the date of issue of any certificate or other document which states that the domestic sub-contract works are practically complete or the date of determination of the employment of theContractor as referred to in clause 22·3·1, whichever is the earlier.

22A Erection of new buildings – All Risks Insurance of the Works by the Contractor [cc]

New buildings – Contractor to take out and maintain a Joint Names Policy for All Risks Insurance

22A·1 The Contractor shall take out and maintain a Joint Names Policy for All Risks Insurance for cover no less than that defined in clause 22·2 [dd] [ff] for the full reinstatement value of the Works (plus the percentage, if any, to cover professional fees stated in the Appendix) and shall (subject to clause 18·1·3) maintain such Joint Names Policy up to and including the date of issue of the certificate of Practical Completion or up to and including the date of determination of the employment of the Contractor under clause 27 or clause 28 or clause 28A (whether or not the validity of that determination is contested), whichever is the earlier.

Where the Employer's status for VAT purposes is exempt or partially exempt the full reinstatement value to which this clause refers shall be inclusive of any VAT on the supply of the work and materials referred to in clause 22A·4·3 for which the Contractor is chargeable by the Commissioners.

Single policy – insurers approved by Employer – failure by Contractor to insure

22A·2 The Joint Names Policy referred to in clause 22A·1 shall be taken out with insurers approved by the Employer, and the Contractor shall send to the Architect for deposit with the Employer that Policy and the premium receipt therefor and also any relevant endorsement or endorsements thereof as may be required to comply with the obligation to maintain that Policy set out in clause 22A·1 and the premium receipts therefor. If the Contractor defaults in taking out or in maintaining the Joint Names Policy as required by clauses 22A·1 and 22A·2 the Employer may himself take out and maintain a Joint Names Policy against any risk in respect of which the default shall have occurred and a sum or sums equivalent to the amount paid or payable by him in respect of premiums therefor may be deducted by him from any monies due or to become due to the Contractor under this Contract or such amount may be recoverable by the Employer from the Contractor as a debt.

Footnote

[ff] In some cases it may not be possible for insurance to be taken out against certain of the risks covered by the definition of 'All Risks Insurance'. This matter should be arranged between the parties prior to entering into the Contract and either the definition of 'All Risks Insurance' given in clause 22·2 amended or the risks actually covered should replace this definition; in the latter case clause 22A·1, clause 22A·3 or clause 22B·1, whichever is applicable, and other relevant clauses in which the definition 'All Risks Insurance' is used should be amended to include the words used to replace this definition.

Use of annual policy maintained by Contractor – alternative to use of clause 22A·2	**22A·3**	·1	If the Contractor independently of his obligations under this Contract maintains a policy of insurance which provides *(inter alia)* All Risks Insurance for cover no less than that defined in clause 22·2 for the full reinstatement value of the Works (plus the percentage, if any, to cover professional fees stated in the Appendix) then the maintenance by the Contractor of such policy shall, if the policy is a Joint Names Policy in respect of the aforesaid Works, be a discharge of the Contractor's obligation to take out and maintain a Joint Names Policy under clause 22A·1. If and so long as the Contractor is able to send to the Architect for inspection by the Employer as and when he is reasonably required to do so by the Employer documentary evidence that such a policy is being maintained then the Contractor shall be discharged from his obligation under clause 22A·2 to deposit the policy and the premium receipt with the Employer but on any occasion the Employer may (but not unreasonably or vexatiously) require to have sent to the Architect for inspection by the Employer the policy to which clause 22A·3·1 refers and the premium receipts therefor. The annual renewal date, as supplied by the Contractor, of the insurance referred to in clause 22A·3·1 is stated in the Appendix.
	22A·3	·2	The provisions of clause 22A·2 shall apply in regard to any default in taking out or in maintaining insurance under clause 22A·3·1.
Loss or damage to Works – insurance claims – Contractor's obligations – use of insurance monies	**22A·4**	·1	If any loss or damage affecting work executed or any part thereof or any Site Materials is occasioned by any one or more of the risks covered by the Joint Names Policy referred to in clause 22A·1 or clause 22A·2 or clause 22A·3 then, upon discovering the said loss or damage, the Contractor shall forthwith give notice in writing both to the Architect and to the Employer of the extent, nature and location thereof.
	22A·4	·2	The occurrence of such loss or damage shall be disregarded in computing any amounts payable to the Contractor under or by virtue of this Contract.
	22A·4	·3	After any inspection required by the insurers in respect of a claim under the Joint Names Policy referred to in clause 22A·1 or clause 22A·2 or clause 22A·3 has been completed the Contractor with due diligence shall restore such work damaged, replace or repair any such Site Materials which have been lost or damaged, remove and dispose of any debris and proceed with the carrying out and completion of the Works.
	22A·4	·4	The Contractor, for himself and for all Nominated and Domestic Sub-Contractors who are, pursuant to clause 22·3, recognised as an insured under the Joint Names Policy referred to in clause 22A·1 or clause 22A·2 or clause 22A·3, shall authorise the insurers to pay all monies from such insurance in respect of the loss or damage referred to in clause 22A·4·1 to the Employer. The Employer shall pay all such monies (less only the amount properly incurred by the Employer in respect of professional fees but not exceeding the amount arrived at by applying the percentage to cover professional fees stated in the Appendix to the amount of the monies so paid excluding any amount included therein for professional fees) to the Contractor by instalments under certificates of the Architect issued at the Period of Interim Certificates.
	22A·4	·5	The Contractor shall not be entitled to any payment in respect of the restoration, replacement or repair of such loss or damage and (when required) the removal and disposal of debris other than the monies received under the aforesaid insurance.
Terrorism cover – non-availability	**22A·5**	·1	If the insurers named in the Joint Names Policy notify the Contractor or the Employer (the 'Insurers' Notification') that, with effect from a date stated by the insurers (the 'Effective Date'), terrorism cover will cease and will no longer be available, the Contractor shall immediately so inform the Employer or the Employer shall immediately so inform the Contractor.
Employer's options	**22A·5**	·2	The Employer, after receipt of the Insurers' Notification but before the Effective Date, shall give notice to the Contractor in writing:

either

·2 ·1 that on and from the Effective Date clause 22A·5·3 shall apply in respect of physical loss or damage to work executed and/or Site Materials due to fire or explosion caused by terrorism;

or

22A·5 *continued*

·2 ·2 that on a date stated by the Employer in his notice (which date shall be after the date of the Insurers' Notification and on or before the Effective Date) the employment of the Contractor under this Contract shall be and is determined; and that upon such determination the provisions of this Contract which require any further payment or any release or any further release of Retention to the Contractor shall not apply and the provisions of clauses 28A·3, 28A·4 and 28A·5 (except clause 28A·5·5) and, where relevant, clause 28A·7 shall thereupon apply.

22A·5 ·3 Where clause 22A·5·2·1 applies then if work executed and/or Site Materials suffer physical loss or damage due to fire or explosion caused by terrorism the Contractor shall with due diligence restore such work damaged, replace or repair any such Site Materials which have been lost or damaged, remove and dispose of any debris and proceed with the carrying out of the Works; and the restoration, replacement or repair of such loss or damage and (when required) the removal and disposal of debris shall be treated as if they were a Variation required by an instruction of the Architect under clause 13·2. The Employer shall not reduce any amount payable to the Contractor pursuant to this clause 22A·5·3 by reason of any act or neglect of the Contractor or of any sub-contractor which may have, or is alleged by the Employer to have, contributed to the physical loss or damage to which this clause refers.

Premium rate changes – terrorism cover

22A·5 ·4 ·1 If the rate on which the premium is based for terrorism cover required under the Joint Names Policy to which clause 22A·1 or clause 22A·3·1 refers is varied at any renewal of the cover, the Contract Sum shall be adjusted by the net amount of the difference in the premium paid by the Contractor as compared to the premium that would have been paid but for the change in the rate.

·4 ·2 Where the Employer is a local authority the Employer may, in lieu of any adjustment of the Contract Sum under clause 22A·5·4·1, instruct the Contractor not to renew the terrorism cover under the Joint Names Policy to which clause 22A·1 or clause 22A·3·1 refers, and state that from the Effective Date the provisions in clause 22A·5·3 shall apply if work executed and/or Site Materials suffer physical loss or damage by fire or explosion caused by terrorism.

22B Erection of new buildings – All Risks Insurance of the Works by the Employer [cc]

New buildings – Employer to take out and maintain a Joint Names Policy for All Risks Insurance

22B·1 The Employer shall take out and maintain a Joint Names Policy for All Risks Insurance for cover no less than that defined in clause 22·2 [dd] [ff] for the full reinstatement value of the Works (plus the percentage, if any, to cover professional fees stated in the Appendix) and shall (subject to clause 18·1·3) maintain such Joint Names Policy up to and including the date of issue of the certificate of Practical Completion or up to and including the date of determination of the employment of the Contractor under clause 27 or clause 28 or clause 28A (whether or not the validity of that determination is contested), whichever is the earlier.

Where the Employer's status for VAT purposes is exempt or partially exempt the full reinstatement value to which this clause refers shall be inclusive of any VAT on the supply of the work and materials referred to in clause 22B·3·3 for which the Contractor is chargeable by the Commissioners.

Failure of Employer to insure – rights of Contractor

22B·2 The Employer shall, as and when reasonably required to do so by the Contractor, produce documentary evidence and receipts showing that the Joint Names Policy required under clause 22B·1 has been taken out and is being maintained. If the Employer defaults in taking out or in maintaining the Joint Names Policy required under clause 22B·1 then the Contractor may himself take out and maintain a Joint Names Policy against any risk in respect of which a default shall have occurred and a sum or sums equivalent to the amount paid or payable by him in respect of the premiums therefor shall be added to the Contract Sum.

Loss or damage to Works – insurance claims – Contractor's obligations – payment by Employer

22B·3 ·1 If any loss or damage affecting work executed or any part thereof or any Site Materials is occasioned by any one or more of the risks covered by the Joint Names Policy referred to in clause 22B·1 or clause 22B·2 then, upon discovering the said loss or damage, the Contractor shall forthwith give notice in writing both to the Architect and to the Employer of the extent, nature and location thereof.

22B·3 ·2 The occurrence of such loss or damage shall be disregarded in computing any amounts payable to the Contractor under or by virtue of this Contract.

22B·3 ·3 After any inspection required by the insurers in respect of a claim under the Joint Names Policy referred to in clause 22B·1 or clause 22B·2 has been completed the Contractor with due diligence shall restore such work damaged, replace or repair any such Site Materials which have been lost or damaged, remove and dispose of any debris and proceed with the carrying out and completion of the Works.

22B·3 ·4 The Contractor, for himself and for all Nominated and Domestic Sub-Contractors who are, pursuant to clause 22·3, recognised as an insured under the Joint Names Policy referred to in clause 22B·1 or clause 22B·2, shall authorise the insurers to pay all monies from such insurance in respect of the loss or damage referred to in clause 22B·3·1 to the Employer.

22B·3 ·5 The restoration, replacement or repair of such loss or damage and (when required) the removal and disposal of debris shall be treated as if they were a Variation required by an instruction of the Architect under clause 13·2.

Terrorism cover – non-availability

22B·4 ·1 If the insurers named in the Joint Names Policy notify the Employer or the Contractor (the 'Insurers' Notification') that, with effect from a date stated by the insurers (the 'Effective Date'), terrorism cover will cease and will no longer be available, the Employer shall immediately so inform the Contractor or the Contractor shall immediately so inform the Employer.

Employer's options

22B·4 ·2 The Employer, after receipt of the Insurers' Notification but before the Effective Date, shall give notice to the Contractor in writing:

either

·2 ·1 that on and from the Effective Date clause 22B·4·3 shall apply in respect of physical loss or damage to work executed and Site Materials due to fire or explosion caused by terrorism;

or

·2 ·2 that on a date stated by the Employer in his notice (which date shall be after the date of the Insurers' Notification and on or before the Effective Date) the employment of the Contractor shall be and is determined; and that upon such determination the provisions of this Contract which require any further payment or any release or any further release of Retention to the Contractor shall not apply and the provisions of clauses 28A·3, 28A·4 and 28A·5 (except clause 28A·5·5) and, where relevant, clause 28A·7 shall thereupon apply.

22B·4 ·3 Where clause 22B·4·2·1 applies then if work executed and/or Site Materials suffer physical loss or damage due to fire or explosion caused by terrorism the Contractor shall with due diligence restore such work damaged, replace or repair any such Site Materials which have been lost or damaged, remove and dispose of any debris and proceed with the carrying out of the Works; and the restoration, replacement or repair of such loss or damage and (when required) the removal and disposal of debris shall be treated as if they were a Variation required by an instruction of the Architect under clause 13·2. The Employer shall not reduce any amount payable to the Contractor pursuant to this clause 22B·4·3 by reason of any act or neglect of the Contractor or of any sub-contractor which may have, or is alleged by the Employer to have, contributed to the physical loss or damage to which this clause refers.

22C Insurance of existing structures – insurance of Works in or extensions to existing structures [cc]

Existing structures and contents – Specified Perils – Employer to take out and maintain Joint Names Policy

22C·1 The Employer shall take out and maintain a Joint Names Policy in respect of the existing structures (which shall include from the relevant date any relevant part to which clause 18·1·3 refers) together with the contents thereof owned by him or for which he is responsible, for the full cost of reinstatement, repair or replacement of loss or damage due to one or more of the Specified Perils [gg] up to and including the date of issue of the certificate of Practical Completion or up to and including the date of determination of the employment of the Contractor under clause 22C·4·3 or clause 27 or clause 28 or clause 28A (whether or not the validity of that determination is contested), whichever is the earlier. The Contractor, for himself and for all Nominated Sub-Contractors who are, pursuant to clause 22·3·1, recognised as an insured under the Joint Names Policy referred to in clause 22C·1 or clause

---

See next page for footnote [**gg**].

22C·1 *continued*

22C·3, shall authorise the insurers to pay all monies from such insurance in respect of loss or damage to the Employer. [hh]

Where the Employer's status for VAT purposes is exempt or partially exempt the full cost of reinstatement, repair or replacement of loss or damage to which this clause refers shall be inclusive of any VAT chargeable on the supply of such reinstatement, repair or replacement.

Terrorism cover – existing structures and contents – non-availability – Employer's options

22C·1 A·1 If the insurers named in the clause 22C·1 Policy notify the Employer or the Contractor (the 'Insurers' Notification') that, with effect from a date stated by the insurers (the 'Effective Date'), terrorism cover under the clause 22C·1 Policy will cease and will no longer be available, the Employer shall immediately so inform the Contractor or the Contractor shall immediately so inform the Employer. The Employer, after receipt of the Insurers' Notification but before the Effective Date, shall give notice to the Contractor in writing:

either

A·1 ·1 that on and from the Effective Date clause 22C·1A·2 shall apply if loss or damage occurs to the structures and/or the contents due to fire or explosion caused by terrorism;

or

A·1 ·2 that on a date stated by the Employer in his notice (which date shall be after the date of the Insurers' Notification and on or before the Effective Date) the employment of the Contractor under this Contract shall be and is determined.

22C·1 A·2 Where clause 22C·1A·1·1 applies, the Employer shall continue to require the Works to be carried out notwithstanding that the existing structures and/or the contents thereof owned by him or for which the Employer is responsible suffer loss or damage due to fire or explosion caused by terrorism; provided that this clause 22C·1A·2 shall not be construed so as to impose an obligation on the Employer to reinstate the existing structures after such loss or damage caused by terrorism.

22C·1 A·3 Where under clause 22C·1A·1·2 the employment of the Contractor under this Contract is determined, then upon such determination the provisions of this Contract which require any payment or any release or any further release of Retention to the Contractor shall not apply and the provisions of clauses 28A·3, 28A·4 and 28A·5 (except clause 28A·5·5) and, where relevant, clause 28A·7 shall thereupon apply.

Works in or extensions to existing structures – All Risks Insurance – Employer to take out and maintain Joint Names Policy

22C·2 The Employer shall take out and maintain a Joint Names Policy for All Risks Insurance for cover no less than that defined in clause 22·2 [dd] [gg] for the full reinstatement value of the Works (plus the percentage, if any, to cover professional fees stated in the Appendix) and shall (subject to clause 18·1·3) maintain such Joint Names Policy up to and including the date of issue of the certificate of Practical Completion or up to and including the date of determination of the employment of the Contractor under clause 22C·4·3 or clause 27 or clause 28 or clause 28A (whether or not the validity of that determination is contested), whichever is the earlier.

Where the Employer's status for VAT purposes is exempt or partially exempt the full reinstatement value to which this clause refers shall be inclusive of any VAT on the supply of the work and materials referred to in clause 22C·4·4·1 for which the Contractor is chargeable by the Commissioners.

Failure of Employer to insure – rights of Contractor

22C·3 The Employer shall, as and when reasonably required to do so by the Contractor, produce documentary evidence and receipts showing that the Joint Names Policy required under clause 22C·1 or clause 22C·2 has been taken out and is being maintained. If the Employer defaults in taking out or in maintaining the Joint Names Policy required under clause 22C·1 the Contractor may himself take out and maintain a Joint Names Policy against any risk in respect of which the default shall have occurred and for that purpose shall have such right

---

Footnotes

[gg] In some cases it may not be possible for insurance to be taken out against certain of the Specified Perils or the risks covered by the definition of 'All Risks Insurance'. This matter should be arranged between the parties prior to entering into the Contract and either the definitions of Specified Perils and/or All Risks Insurance given in clauses 1·3 and 22·2 amended or the risks actually covered should replace the definitions; in the latter case clause 22C·1 and/or clause 22C·2 and other relevant clauses in which the definitions 'All Risks Insurance' and/or 'Specified Perils' are used should be amended to include the words used to replace those definitions.

[hh] Some Employers e.g. tenants may not be able to fulfil the obligations in clause 22C·1. If so clause 22C·1 should be amended accordingly.

22C·3 *continued*

of entry and inspection as may be required to make a survey and inventory of the existing structures and the relevant contents. If the Employer defaults in taking out or in maintaining the Joint Names Policy required under clause 22C·2 the Contractor may take out and maintain a Joint Names Policy against any risk in respect of which the default shall have occurred. A sum or sums equivalent to the premiums paid or payable by the Contractor pursuant to clause 22C·3 shall be added to the Contract Sum.

Loss or damage to Works – insurance claims – Contractor's obligations – payment by Employer

22C·4 If any loss or damage affecting work executed or any part thereof or any Site Materials is occasioned by any one or more of the risks covered by the Joint Names Policy referred to in clause 22C·2 or clause 22C·3 then, upon discovering the said loss or damage, the Contractor shall forthwith give notice in writing both to the Architect and to the Employer of the extent, nature and location thereof and

22C·4 ·1 the occurrence of such loss or damage shall be disregarded in computing any amounts payable to the Contractor under or by virtue of this Contract;

22C·4 ·2 the Contractor, for himself and for all Nominated and Domestic Sub-Contractors who are, pursuant to clause 22·3, recognised as an insured under the Joint Names Policy referred to in clause 22C·2 or clause 22C·3, shall authorise the insurers to pay all monies from such insurance in respect of the loss or damage referred to in clause 22C·4 to the Employer;

22C·4 ·3 ·1 if it is just and equitable so to do the employment of the Contractor under this Contract may within 28 days of the occurrence of such loss or damage be determined at the option of either Party by notice by special delivery or recorded delivery from either Party to the other. Within 7 days of receiving such a notice (but not thereafter) either Party may invoke the relevant procedures applicable under the Contract to the resolution of disputes or differences in order that it may be decided whether such determination is just and equitable;

·3 ·2 upon the giving or receiving by the Employer of a notice of determination, or where the relevant procedures referred to in clause 22C·4·3·1 have been invoked and the notice of determination has been upheld, the provisions of clauses 28A·4 and 28A·5 (except clause 28A·5·5) shall apply.

22C·4 ·4 If no notice of determination is served under clause 22C·4·3·1, or where the relevant procedures referred to in clause 22C·4·3·1 have been invoked and the notice of determination has not been upheld, then

·4 ·1 after any inspection required by the insurers in respect of a claim under the Joint Names Policy referred to in clause 22C·2 or clause 22C·3 has been completed, the Contractor with due diligence shall restore such work damaged, replace or repair any such Site Materials which have been lost or damaged, remove and dispose of any debris and proceed with the carrying out and completion of the Works; and

·4 ·2 the restoration, replacement or repair of such loss or damage and (when required) the removal and disposal of debris shall be treated as if they were a Variation required by an instruction of the Architect under clause 13·2.

Terrorism cover – non-availability

22C·5 ·1 If the insurers named in the Joint Names Policy notify the Employer or the Contractor (the 'Insurers' Notification') that, with effect from a date stated by the insurers (the 'Effective Date'), terrorism cover will cease and will no longer be available, the Employer shall immediately so inform the Contractor or the Contractor shall immediately so inform the Employer.

Employer's options

22C·5 ·2 The Employer, after receipt of the Insurers' Notification but before the Effective Date, shall give notice to the Contractor in writing:

either

·2 ·1 that on and from the Effective Date clause 22C·5·3 shall apply in respect of physical loss or damage to work executed and Site Materials due to fire or explosion caused by terrorism;

or

22C·5 *continued*

·2 ·2 that on a date stated by the Employer in his notice (which date shall be after the date of the Insurers' Notification and on or before the Effective Date) the employment of the Contractor shall be and is determined; and that upon such determination the provisions of this Contract which require any further payment or any release or any further release of Retention to the Contractor shall not apply and the provisions of clauses 28A·3, 28A·4 and 28A·5 (except clause 28A·5·5) shall thereupon apply.

22C·5 ·3 Where clause 22C·5·2·1 applies then if work executed and/or Site Materials suffer physical loss or damage due to fire or explosion caused by terrorism the Contractor shall with due diligence restore such work damaged, replace or repair any such Site Materials which have been lost or damaged, remove and dispose of any debris and proceed with the carrying out of the Works; and the restoration, replacement or repair of such loss or damage and (when required) the removal and disposal of any debris shall be treated as if they were a Variation required by an instruction of the Architect under clause 13·2. The Employer shall not reduce any amount payable to the Contractor pursuant to this clause 22C·5·3 by reason of any act or neglect of the Contractor or of any sub-contractor which may have, or is alleged by the Employer to have, contributed to the physical loss or damage to which this clause refers.

22D Insurance for Employer's loss of liquidated damages – clause 25·4·3

22D·1 Where it is stated in the Appendix that the insurance to which clause 22D refers may be required by the Employer then forthwith after the Contract has been entered into the Architect shall either inform the Contractor that no such insurance is required or instruct the Contractor to obtain a quotation for such insurance. This quotation shall be for an insurance on an agreed value basis [ii] to be taken out and maintained by the Contractor until the date of Practical Completion and which will provide for payment to the Employer of a sum calculated by reference to clause 22D·3 in the event of loss or damage to the Works, work executed, Site Materials, temporary buildings, plant and equipment for use in connection with and on or adjacent to the Works by any one or more of the Specified Perils and which loss or damage results in the Architect giving an extension of time under clause 25·3 in respect of the Relevant Event in clause 25·4·3. The Architect shall obtain from the Employer any information which the Contractor reasonably requires to obtain such quotation. The Contractor shall send to the Architect as soon as practicable the quotation which he has obtained and the Architect shall thereafter instruct the Contractor whether or not the Employer wishes the Contractor to accept that quotation and such instruction shall not be unreasonably delayed or withheld. If the Contractor is instructed to accept the quotation the Contractor shall forthwith take out and maintain the relevant policy and send it to the Architect for deposit with the Employer, together with the premium receipt therefor and also any relevant endorsement or endorsements thereof and the premium receipts therefor.

22D·2 The sum insured by the relevant policy shall be a sum calculated at the rate stated in the Appendix as liquidated and ascertained damages for the period of time stated in the Appendix.

22D·3 Payment in respect of this insurance shall be calculated at the rate referred to in clause 22D·2 (or any revised rate produced by the application of clause 18·1·4) for the period of any extension of time finally given by the Architect as referred to in clause 22D·1 or for the period of time stated in the Appendix, whichever is the less.

22D·4 The amounts expended by the Contractor to take out and maintain the insurance referred to in clause 22D·1 shall be added to the Contract Sum. If the Contractor defaults in taking out or in maintaining the insurance referred to in clause 22D·1 the Employer may himself insure against any risk in respect of which the default shall have occurred.

Footnote

[ii] The adoption of an agreed value is to avoid any dispute over the amount of the payment due under the insurance once the policy is issued. Insurers on receiving a proposal for the insurance to which clause 22D refers will normally reserve the right to be satisfied that the sum referred to in clause 22D·2 is not more than a genuine pre-estimate of the damages which the Employer considers, at the time he enters into the Contract, he will suffer as a result of any delay.

22FC Joint Fire Code – compliance

Application of clause

22FC ·1 Clause 22FC applies where it is stated in the Appendix that the Joint Fire Code applies.

Compliance with Joint Fire Code

22FC ·2 ·1 The Employer shall comply with the Joint Fire Code and ensure such compliance by his servants or agents and by any person employed, engaged or authorised by him upon or in connection with the Works or any part thereof other than the Contractor and the persons for whom the Contractor is responsible pursuant to clause 22FC·2·2.

·2 ·2 The Contractor shall comply with the Joint Fire Code and ensure such compliance by his servants or agents or by any person employed or engaged by him upon or in connection with the Works or any part thereof their servants or agents or by any other person who may properly be on the site upon or in connection with the Works or any part thereof other than the Employer or any person employed, engaged or authorised by him or by any local authority or statutory undertaker executing work solely in pursuance of its statutory rights or obligations.

Breach of Joint Fire Code – Remedial Measures

22FC ·3 ·1 If a breach of the Joint Fire Code occurs and the insurers under the Joint Names Policy in respect of the Works specify by notice to the Employer or the Contractor the remedial measures they require (the 'Remedial Measures') and the time by which such Remedial Measures are to be completed (the 'Remedial Measures Completion Date'), the Party receiving the notice shall copy the notice to the other and the Employer shall copy such notice to the Architect; and then:

22FC ·3 ·1 ·1 subject to clause 22FC·3·1·2, where the Remedial Measures relate to the obligation of the Contractor to carry out and complete the Works the Contractor shall ensure that the Remedial Measures are carried out by the Remedial Measures Completion Date;

·1 ·2 to the extent that the Remedial Measures require a Variation to the Works as described in the Contract Documents, in the Numbered Documents or in an Architect's instruction, the Architect shall issue such instructions as are necessary to enable compliance. If, in any emergency, compliance with the Remedial Measures in whole or in part requires the Contractor to supply materials or execute work before receiving instructions under this clause, the Contractor shall supply such limited materials and execute such limited work as are reasonably necessary to secure immediate compliance. The Contractor shall forthwith inform the Architect of the emergency and of the steps he is taking under this clause. Such work executed and materials supplied by the Contractor shall be treated as if they had been executed and supplied under an Architect's instruction requiring a Variation.

22FC ·3 ·2 If the Contractor, within 7 days of receipt of a notice specifying Remedial Measures not requiring an Architect's instruction under 22FC·3·1·2, does not begin to carry out or thereafter fails without reasonable cause regularly and diligently to proceed with the Remedial Measures, then the Employer may employ and pay other persons to carry out those Remedial Measures; and all costs incurred in connection with such employment may be withheld and/or deducted by him from any monies due or to become due to the Contractor or may be recoverable from the Contractor by the Employer as a debt.

22FC ·4 [Number not used]

Joint Fire Code – amendments/ revisions

22FC ·5 If after the Base Date the Joint Fire Code is amended/revised and the Joint Fire Code as amended/revised is, under the Joint Names Policy, applicable to the Works, the cost, if any, of compliance by the Contractor with any amendment(s)/ revision(s) to the Joint Fire Code shall, as stated in the Appendix, be borne either by the Employer and added to the Contract Sum or by the Contractor.

23 Date of Possession, completion and postponement

Date of Possession – progress to Completion Date

23·1 ·1 On the Date of Possession possession of the site shall be given to the Contractor who shall thereupon begin the Works and regularly and diligently proceed with the same and shall complete the same on or before the Completion Date.

23·1   ·2 Where clause 23·1·2 is stated in the Appendix to apply the Employer may defer the giving of possession for a period not exceeding six weeks or such lesser period stated in the Appendix calculated from the Date of Possession.

Architect's instructions – postponement

23·2 The Architect may issue instructions in regard to the postponement of any work to be executed under the provisions of this Contract.

Possession by Contractor – use or occupation by Employer

23·3   ·1 For the purposes of the Works insurances the Contractor shall retain possession of the site and the Works up to and including the date of issue of the certificate of Practical Completion, and, subject to clause 18, the Employer shall not be entitled to take possession of any part or parts of the Works until that date.

23·3   ·2 Notwithstanding the provisions of clause 23·3·1 the Employer may, with the consent in writing of the Contractor, use or occupy the site or the Works or part thereof whether for the purposes of storage of his goods or otherwise before the date of issue of the certificate of Practical Completion by the Architect. Before the Contractor shall give his consent to such use or occupation the Contractor or the Employer shall notify the insurers under clause 22A or clause 22B or clause 22C·2 to ·4 whichever may be applicable and obtain confirmation that such use or occupation will not prejudice the insurance. Subject to such confirmation the consent of the Contractor shall not be unreasonably delayed or withheld.

23·3   ·3 Where clause 22A·1 or clause 22A·3 applies and the insurers in giving the confirmation referred to in clause 23·3·2 have made it a condition of such confirmation that an additional premium is required the Contractor shall notify the Employer of the amount of the additional premium. If the Employer continues to require use or occupation under clause 23·3·2 the additional premium required shall be added to the Contract Sum and the Contractor shall provide the Employer, if so requested, with the additional premium receipt therefor.

24 Damages for non-completion

Certificate of Architect

24·1 If the Contractor fails to complete the Works by the Completion Date then the Architect shall issue a certificate to that effect. In the event of a new Completion Date being fixed after the issue of such a certificate such fixing shall cancel that certificate and the Architect shall issue such further certificate under clause 24·1 as may be necessary.

Payment or allowance of liquidated damages

24·2   ·1 Provided:

– the Architect has issued a certificate under clause 24·1; and

– the Employer has informed the Contractor in writing before the date of the Final Certificate that he may require payment of, or may withhold or deduct, liquidated and ascertained damages,

then the Employer may, not later than 5 days before the final date for payment of the debt due under the Final Certificate:

either

  ·1 ·1 require in writing the Contractor to pay to the Employer liquidated and ascertained damages at the rate stated in the Appendix (or at such lesser rate as may be specified in writing by the Employer) for the period between the Completion Date and the date of Practical Completion and the Employer may recover the same as a debt;

or

  ·1 ·2 give a notice pursuant to clause 30·1·1·4 or clause 30·8·3 to the Contractor that he will deduct from monies due to the Contractor liquidated and ascertained damages at the rate stated in the Appendix (or at such lesser rate as may be specified in the notice) for the period between the Completion Date and the date of Practical Completion.

24·2   ·2 If, under clause 25·3·3, the Architect fixes a later Completion Date or a later Completion Date is stated in a confirmed acceptance of a 13A Quotation, the Employer shall pay or repay to the Contractor any amounts recovered, allowed or paid under clause 24·2·1 for the period up to such later Completion Date.

24·2 ·3 Notwithstanding the issue of any further certificate of the Architect under clause 24·1 any requirement of the Employer which has been previously stated in writing in accordance with clause 24·2·1 shall remain effective unless withdrawn by the Employer.

25 Extension of time [jj]

Interpretation of delay

25·1 In clause 25 any reference to delay, notice or extension of time includes further delay, further notice or further extension of time.

Notice by Contractor of delay to progress

25·2 ·1 ·1 If and whenever it becomes reasonably apparent that the progress of the Works is being or is likely to be delayed the Contractor shall forthwith give written notice to the Architect of the material circumstances including the cause or causes of the delay and identify in such notice any event which in his opinion is a Relevant Event.

·1 ·2 Where the material circumstances of which written notice has been given under clause 25·2·1·1 include reference to a Nominated Sub-Contractor, the Contractor shall forthwith send a copy of such written notice to the Nominated Sub-Contractor concerned.

25·2 ·2 In respect of each and every Relevant Event identified in the notice given in accordance with clause 25·2·1·1 the Contractor shall, if practicable in such notice, or otherwise in writing as soon as possible after such notice:

·2 ·1 give particulars of the expected effects thereof; and

·2 ·2 estimate the extent, if any, of the expected delay in the completion of the Works beyond the Completion Date resulting therefrom whether or not concurrently with delay resulting from any other Relevant Event

and shall give such particulars and estimate to any Nominated Sub-Contractor to whom a copy of any written notice has been given under clause 25·2·1·2.

25·2 ·3 The Contractor shall give such further written notices to the Architect, and send a copy to any Nominated Sub-Contractor to whom a copy of any written notice has been given under clause 25·2·1·2, as may be reasonably necessary or as the Architect may reasonably require for keeping up-to-date the particulars and estimate referred to in clauses 25·2·2·1 and 25·2·2·2 including any material change in such particulars or estimate.

Fixing Completion Date

25·3 ·1 If, in the opinion of the Architect, upon receipt of any notice, particulars and estimate under clauses 25·2·1·1, 25·2·2 and 25·2·3.

·1 ·1 any of the events which are stated by the Contractor to be the cause of the delay is a Relevant Event and

·1 ·2 the completion of the Works is likely to be delayed thereby beyond the Completion Date

the Architect shall in writing to the Contractor give an extension of time by fixing such later date as the Completion Date as he then estimates to be fair and reasonable. The Architect shall, in fixing such new Completion Date, state:

·1 ·3 which of the Relevant Events he has taken into account and

·1 ·4 the extent, if any, to which he has had regard to any instructions issued under clause 13·2 which require as a Variation the omission of any work or obligation and/or under clause 13·3 in regard to the expenditure of a provisional sum for defined work or for Performance Specified Work which results in the omission of any such work,

and shall, if reasonably practicable having regard to the sufficiency of the aforesaid notice, particulars and estimate, fix such new Completion Date not later than 12 weeks from receipt of the notice and of reasonably sufficient particulars and estimate, or, where the period between receipt thereof and the Completion Date is less than 12 weeks, not later than the Completion Date.

Footnote [jj] See clauses 38·4·7, 39·5·7 and 40·7 (restriction of fluctuations or price adjustment during period where Contractor is in default over completion).

25·3 ·1 *continued*

If, in the opinion of the Architect, upon receipt of any such notice, particulars and estimate, it is not fair and reasonable to fix a later date as a new Completion Date, the Architect shall if reasonably practicable having regard to the sufficiency of the aforesaid notice, particulars and estimate so notify the Contractor in writing not later than 12 weeks from receipt of the notice, particulars and estimate, or, where the period between receipt thereof and the Completion Date is less than 12 weeks, not later than the Completion Date.

25·3 ·2 After the first exercise by the Architect of his duty under clause 25·3·1 or after any revision to the Completion Date stated by the Architect in a confirmed acceptance of a 13A Quotation in respect of a Variation the Architect may in writing fix a Completion Date earlier than that previously fixed under clause 25 or than that stated by the Architect in a confirmed acceptance of a 13A Quotation if in his opinion the fixing of such earlier Completion Date is fair and reasonable having regard to any instructions issued after the last occasion on which the Architect fixed a new Completion Date

- under clause 13·2 which require or sanction as a Variation the omission of any work or obligation; and/or

- under clause 13·3 in regard to the expenditure of a provisional sum for defined work or for Performance Specified Work which result in the omission of any such work.

Provided that no decision under clause 25·3·2 shall alter the length of any adjustment to the time required by the Contractor for the completion of the Works in respect of a Variation for which a 13A Quotation has been given and which has been stated in a confirmed acceptance of a 13A Quotation or in respect of a Variation or work for which an adjustment to the time for completion of the Works has been accepted pursuant to clause 13·4·1·2 paragraph A7.

25·3 ·3 After the Completion Date, if this occurs before the date of Practical Completion, the Architect may, and not later than the expiry of 12 weeks after the date of Practical Completion shall, in writing to the Contractor either

·3 ·1 fix a Completion Date later than that previously fixed if in his opinion the fixing of such later Completion Date is fair and reasonable having regard to any of the Relevant Events, whether upon reviewing a previous decision or otherwise and whether or not the Relevant Event has been specifically notified by the Contractor under clause 25·2·1·1; or

·3 ·2 fix a Completion Date earlier than that previously fixed under clause 25 or stated in a confirmed acceptance of a 13A Quotation if in his opinion the fixing of such earlier Completion Date is fair and reasonable having regard to any instructions issued after the last occasion on which the Architect fixed a new Completion Date

- under clause 13·2 which require or sanction as a Variation the omission of any work or obligation; and/or

- under clause 13·3 in regard to the expenditure of a provisional sum for defined work or for Performance Specified Work which result in the omission of any such work; or

·3 ·3 confirm to the Contractor the Completion Date previously fixed or stated in a confirmed acceptance of a 13A Quotation.

Provided that no decision under clause 25·3·3·1 or clause 25·3·3·2 shall alter the length of any adjustment to the time required by the Contractor for the completion of the Works in respect of a Variation for which a 13A Quotation has been given and which has been stated in a confirmed acceptance of a 13A Quotation.

25·3 ·4 Provided always that:

·4 ·1 the Contractor shall use constantly his best endeavours to prevent delay in the progress of the Works, howsoever caused, and to prevent the completion of the Works being delayed or further delayed beyond the Completion Date;

·4 ·2 the Contractor shall do all that may reasonably be required to the satisfaction of the Architect to proceed with the Works.

25·3 **·5** The Architect shall notify in writing to every Nominated Sub-Contractor each decision of the Architect under clause 25·3 fixing a Completion Date and each revised Completion Date stated in the confirmed acceptance of a 13A Quotation together with, where relevant, any revised period or periods for the completion of the work of each Nominated Sub-Contractor stated in such confirmed acceptance.

25·3 **·6** No decision of the Architect under clause 25·3·2 or clause 25·3·3·2 shall fix a Completion Date earlier than the Date for Completion stated in the Appendix.

Relevant Events **25·4** The following are the Relevant Events referred to in clause 25:

25·4 **·1** force majeure;

25·4 **·2** exceptionally adverse weather conditions;

25·4 **·3** loss or damage occasioned by any one or more of the Specified Perils;

25·4 **·4** civil commotion, local combination of workmen, strike or lock-out affecting any of the trades employed upon the Works or any of the trades engaged in the preparation, manufacture or transportation of any of the goods or materials required for the Works;

25·4 **·5** compliance with the Architect's instructions

·5 ·1 under clauses 2·3, 2·4·1, 13·2 (except for a confirmed acceptance of a 13A Quotation), 13·3 (except compliance with an Architect's instruction for the expenditure of a provisional sum for defined work or of a provisional sum for Performance Specified Work), 13A·4·1, 23·2, 34, 35 or 36; or

·5 ·2 in regard to the opening up for inspection of any work covered up or the testing of any of the work, materials or goods in accordance with clause 8·3 (including making good in consequence of such opening up or testing) unless the inspection or test showed that the work, materials or goods were not in accordance with this Contract;

25·4 **·6** **·1** where an Information Release Schedule has been provided, failure of the Architect to comply with clause 5·4·1;

·6 ·2 failure of the Architect to comply with clause 5·4·2;

25·4 **·7** delay on the part of Nominated Sub-Contractors or Nominated Suppliers which the Contractor has taken all practicable steps to avoid or reduce;

25·4 **·8** **·1** the execution of work not forming part of this Contract by the Employer himself or by persons employed or otherwise engaged by the Employer as referred to in clause 29 or the failure to execute such work;

·8 ·2 the supply by the Employer of materials and goods which the Employer has agreed to provide for the Works or the failure so to supply;

25·4 **·9** the exercise after the Base Date by the United Kingdom Government of any statutory power which directly affects the execution of the Works by restricting the availability or use of labour which is essential to the proper carrying out of the Works or preventing the Contractor from, or delaying the Contractor in, securing such goods or materials or such fuel or energy as are essential to the proper carrying out of the Works;

25·4 **·10** **·1** the Contractor's inability for reasons beyond his control and which he could not reasonably have foreseen at the Base Date to secure such labour as is essential to the proper carrying out of the Works; or

·10 ·2 the Contractor's inability for reasons beyond his control and which he could not reasonably have foreseen at the Base Date to secure such goods or materials as are essential to the proper carrying out of the Works;

25·4 **·11** the carrying out by a local authority or statutory undertaker of work in pursuance of its statutory obligations in relation to the Works, or the failure to carry out such work;

25·4 ·12 failure of the Employer to give in due time ingress to or egress from the site of the Works or any part thereof through or over any land, buildings, way or passage adjoining or connected with the site and in the possession and control of the Employer, in accordance with the Contract Bills and/or the Contract Drawings, after receipt by the Architect of such notice, if any, as the Contractor is required to give, or failure of the Employer to give such ingress or egress as otherwise agreed between the Architect and the Contractor;

25·4 ·13 where clause 23·1·2 is stated in the Appendix to apply, the deferment by the Employer of giving possession of the site under clause 23·1·2;

25·4 ·14 by reason of the execution of work for which an Approximate Quantity is included in the Contract Bills which is not a reasonably accurate forecast of the quantity of work required;

25·4 ·15 delay which the Contractor has taken all practicable steps to avoid or reduce consequent upon a change in the Statutory Requirements after the Base Date which necessitates some alteration or modification to any Performance Specified Work;

25·4 ·16 the use or threat of terrorism and/or the activity of the relevant authorities in dealing with such use or threat;

25·4 ·17 compliance or non-compliance by the Employer with clause 6A·1;

25·4 ·18 delay arising from a suspension by the Contractor of the performance of his obligations under the Contract to the Employer pursuant to clause 30·1·4;

25·4 ·19 save as provided for in clauses 25·4·1 to 25·4·18 any impediment, prevention or default, whether by act or omission, by the Employer or any person for whom the Employer is responsible except to the extent that it was caused or contributed to by any default, whether by act or omission, of the Contractor or his servants, agents or sub-contractors.

26 Loss and expense caused by matters materially affecting regular progress of the Works

Matters materially affecting regular progress of the Works – direct loss and/or expense

26·1 If the Contractor makes written application to the Architect stating that he has incurred or is likely to incur direct loss and/or expense (of which the Contractor may give his quantification) in the execution of this Contract for which he would not be reimbursed by a payment under any other provision in this Contract due to deferment of giving possession of the site under clause 23·1·2 where clause 23·1·2 is stated in the Appendix to be applicable or because the regular progress of the Works or of any part thereof has been or is likely to be materially affected by any one or more of the matters referred to in clause 26·2; and if and as soon as the Architect is of the opinion that the direct loss and/or expense has been incurred or is likely to be incurred due to any such deferment of giving possession or that the regular progress of the Works or of any part thereof has been or is likely to be so materially affected as set out in the application of the Contractor then the Architect from time to time thereafter shall ascertain, or shall instruct the Quantity Surveyor to ascertain, the amount of such loss and/or expense which has been or is being incurred by the Contractor; provided always that:

26·1 ·1 the Contractor's application shall be made as soon as it has become, or should reasonably have become, apparent to him that the regular progress of the Works or of any part thereof has been or was likely to be affected as aforesaid; and

26·1 ·2 the Contractor shall in support of his application submit to the Architect upon request such information as should reasonably enable the Architect to form an opinion as aforesaid; and

26·1 ·3 the Contractor shall submit to the Architect or to the Quantity Surveyor upon request such details of such loss and/or expense as are reasonably necessary for such ascertainment as aforesaid.

List of matters

26·2 The following are the matters referred to in clause 26·1:

26·2 ·1 ·1 where an Information Release Schedule has been provided, failure of the Architect to comply with clause 5·4·1;

·1 ·2 failure of the Architect to comply with clause 5·4·2;

26·2 ·2 the opening up for inspection of any work covered up or the testing of any of the work, materials or goods in accordance with clause 8·3 (including making good in consequence of such opening up or testing), unless the inspection or test showed that the work, materials or goods were not in accordance with this Contract;

26·2 ·3 any discrepancy in or divergence between the Contract Drawings and/or the Contract Bills and/or the Numbered Documents;

26·2 ·4 ·1 the execution of work not forming part of this Contract by the Employer himself or by persons employed or otherwise engaged by the Employer as referred to in clause 29 or the failure to execute such work;

·4 ·2 the supply by the Employer of materials and goods which the Employer has agreed to provide for the Works or the failure so to supply;

26·2 ·5 Architect's instructions under clause 23·2 issued in regard to the postponement of any work to be executed under the provisions of this Contract;

26·2 ·6 failure of the Employer to give in due time ingress to or egress from the site of the Works or any part thereof through or over any land, buildings, way or passage adjoining or connected with the site and in the possession and control of the Employer, in accordance with the Contract Bills and/or the Contract Drawings, after receipt by the Architect of such notice, if any, as the Contractor is required to give, or failure of the Employer to give such ingress or egress as otherwise agreed between the Architect and the Contractor;

26·2 ·7 Architect's instructions issued

under clause 13·2 or clause 13A·4·1 requiring a Variation (except for a Variation for which the Architect has given a confirmed acceptance of a 13A Quotation or for a Variation thereto) or

under clause 13·3 in regard to the expenditure of provisional sums (other than instructions to which clause 13·4·2 refers or an instruction for the expenditure of a provisional sum for defined work or of a provisional sum for Performance Specified Work);

26·2 ·8 the execution of work for which an Approximate Quantity is included in the Contract Bills which is not a reasonably accurate forecast of the quantity of work required;

26·2 ·9 compliance or non-compliance by the Employer with clause 6A·1;

26·2 ·10 suspension by the Contractor of the performance of his obligations under the Contract to the Employer pursuant to clause 30·1·4 provided the suspension was not frivolous or vexatious;

26·2 ·11 save as provided for in clauses 26·2·1 to 26·2·10 any impediment, prevention or default, whether by act or omission, by the Employer or any person for whom the Employer is responsible except to the extent that it was caused or contributed to by any default, whether by act or omission, of the Contractor or his servants, agents or sub-contractors.

Relevance of certain extensions of Completion Date

26·3 If and to the extent that it is necessary for ascertainment under clause 26·1 of loss and/or expense the Architect shall state in writing to the Contractor what extension of time, if any, has been made under clause 25 in respect of the Relevant Event or Events referred to in clause 25·4·5·1 (so far as that clause refers to clauses 2·3, 13·2, 13·3 and 23·2) and in clauses 25·4·5·2, 25·4·6, 25·4·8 and 25·4·12.

Nominated Sub-Contractors – matters materially affecting regular progress of the sub-contract works – direct loss and/or expense

26·4 ·1 The Contractor upon receipt of a written application properly made by a Nominated Sub-Contractor under clause 4·38·1 of Conditions NSC/C shall pass to the Architect a copy of that written application. If and as soon as the Architect is of the opinion that the loss and/or expense to which the said clause 4·38·1 refers has been incurred or is likely to be incurred due to any deferment of the giving of possession where clause 23·1·2 is stated in the Appendix to apply or that the regular progress of the sub-contract works or of any part thereof has been or is likely to be materially affected as referred to in clause 4·38·1 of Conditions NSC/C and as set out in the application of the Nominated Sub-Contractor then the Architect shall himself ascertain, or shall instruct the Quantity Surveyor to ascertain, the amount of loss and/or expense to which the said clause 4·38·1 refers.

26·4 ·2 If and to the extent that it is necessary for the ascertainment of such loss and/or expense the Architect shall state in writing to the Contractor with a copy to the Nominated Sub-Contractor concerned what was the length of the revision of the period or periods for completion of the sub-contract works or of any part thereof to which he gave consent in respect of the Relevant Event or Events set out in clause 2·6·5·1 (so far as that clause refers to clauses 2·3, 13·2, 13·3 and 23·2 of the Main Contract Conditions), 2·6·5·2, 2·6·6, 2·6·8, 2·6·12 and 2·6·15 of Conditions NSC/C.

Amounts ascertained – added to Contract Sum

26·5 Any amount from time to time ascertained under clause 26 shall be added to the Contract Sum.

Reservation of rights and remedies of Contractor

26·6 The provisions of clause 26 are without prejudice to any other rights and remedies which the Contractor may possess.

27 Determination by Employer

Notices under clause 27

27·1 Any notice or further notice to which clauses 27·2·1, 27·2·2, 27·2·3 and 27·3·4 refer shall be in writing and given by actual delivery or by special delivery or recorded delivery. If sent by special delivery or recorded delivery the notice or further notice shall, subject to proof to the contrary, be deemed to have been received 48 hours after the date of posting (excluding Saturday and Sunday and Public Holidays).

Default by Contractor

27·2 ·1 If, before the date of Practical Completion, the Contractor shall make a default in any one or more of the following respects:

·1 ·1 without reasonable cause he wholly or substantially suspends the carrying out of the Works; or

·1 ·2 he fails to proceed regularly and diligently with the Works; or

·1 ·3 he refuses or neglects to comply with a written notice or instruction from the Architect requiring him to remove any work, materials or goods not in accordance with this Contract and by such refusal or neglect the Works are materially affected; or

·1 ·4 he fails to comply with the provisions of clause 19·1·1 or clause 19·2·2; or

·1 ·5 he fails pursuant to the Conditions to comply with the requirements of the CDM Regulations,

the Architect may give to the Contractor a notice specifying the default or defaults (the 'specified default or defaults').

27·2 ·2 If the Contractor continues a specified default for 14 days from receipt of the notice under clause 27·2·1 then the Employer may on, or within 10 days from, the expiry of that 14 days by a further notice to the Contractor determine the employment of the Contractor under this Contract. Such determination shall take effect on the date of receipt of such further notice.

27·2 ·3 If

the Contractor ends the specified default or defaults, or

the Employer does not give the further notice referred to in clause 27·2·2

and the Contractor repeats a specified default (whether previously repeated or not) then, upon or within a reasonable time after such repetition, the Employer may by notice to the Contractor determine the employment of the Contractor under this Contract. Such determination shall take effect on the date of receipt of such notice.

27·2 ·4 A notice of determination under clause 27·2·2 or clause 27·2·3 shall not be given unreasonably or vexatiously.

Insolvency of Contractor

27·3 ·1 If the Contractor

makes a composition or arrangement with his creditors, or becomes bankrupt, or,

being a company,

makes a proposal for a voluntary arrangement for a composition of debts or scheme of arrangement to be approved in accordance with the Companies Act 1985 or the Insolvency Act 1986 as the case may be or any amendment or re-enactment thereof, or

has a provisional liquidator appointed, or

has a winding-up order made, or

passes a resolution for voluntary winding-up (except for the purposes of amalgamation or reconstruction), or

under the Insolvency Act 1986 or any amendment or re-enactment thereof has an administrator or an administrative receiver appointed

then:

27·3 ·2 the Contractor shall immediately inform the Employer in writing if he has made a composition or arrangement with his creditors, or, being a company, has made a proposal for a voluntary arrangement for a composition of debts or scheme of arrangement to be approved in accordance with the Companies Act 1985 or the Insolvency Act 1986 as the case may be or any amendment or re-enactment thereof;

27·3 ·3 where a provisional liquidator or trustee in bankruptcy is appointed or a winding-up order is made or the Contractor passes a resolution for voluntary winding-up (except for the purposes of amalgamation or reconstruction) the employment of the Contractor under this Contract shall be forthwith automatically determined but the said employment may be reinstated if the Employer and the Contractor [kk] shall so agree;

27·3 ·4 where clause 27·3·3 does not apply the Employer may at any time, unless an agreement to which clause 27·5·2·1 refers has been made, by notice to the Contractor determine the employment of the Contractor under this Contract and such determination shall take effect on the date of receipt of such notice.

Corruption

27·4 The Employer shall be entitled to determine the employment of the Contractor, under this or any other contract, if the Contractor shall have offered or given or agreed to give to any person any gift or consideration of any kind as an inducement or reward for doing or forbearing to do or for having done or forborne to do any action in relation to the obtaining or execution of this or any other contract with the Employer, or for showing or forbearing to show favour or disfavour to any person in relation to this or any other contract with the Employer, or if the like acts shall have been done by any person employed by the Contractor or acting on his behalf (whether with or without the knowledge of the Contractor), or if in relation to this or any other contract with the Employer the Contractor or any person employed by him or acting on his behalf shall have committed an offence under the Prevention of Corruption Acts 1889 to 1916.

Insolvency of Contractor – option to Employer

27·5 Clauses 27·5·1 to 27·5·4 are only applicable where clause 27·3·4 applies.

27·5 ·1 From the date when, under clause 27·3·4, the Employer could first give notice to determine the employment of the Contractor, the Employer, subject to clause 27·5·3, shall not be bound by any provisions of this Contract to make any further payment thereunder and the Contractor shall not be bound to continue to carry out and complete the Works in compliance with clause 2·1.

Footnote

[kk] See JCT Practice Note 24: after certain insolvency events an Insolvency Practitioner acts for the Contractor.

27·5   ·2   Clause 27·5·1 shall apply until

either

    ·2 ·1   the Employer makes an agreement (a '27·5·2·1 agreement') with the Contractor on the continuation or novation or conditional novation of this Contract, in which case this Contract shall be subject to the terms set out in the 27·5·2·1 agreement

or

    ·2 ·2   the Employer determines the employment of the Contractor under this Contract in accordance with clause 27·3·4, in which case the provisions of clause 27·6 or clause 27·7 shall apply.

27·5   ·3   Notwithstanding clause 27·5·1, in the period before either a 27·5·2·1 agreement is made or the Employer under clause 27·3·4 determines the employment of the Contractor, the Employer and the Contractor may make an interim arrangement for work to be carried out. Subject to clause 27·5·4 any right of set-off which the Employer may have shall not be exercisable in respect of any payment due from the Employer to the Contractor under such interim arrangement.

27·5   ·4   From the date when, under clause 27·3·4, the Employer may first determine the employment of the Contractor (but subject to any agreement made pursuant to clause 27·5·2·1 or arrangement made pursuant to clause 27·5·3) the Employer may take reasonable measures to ensure that Site Materials, the site and the Works are adequately protected and that Site Materials are retained in, on the site of or adjacent to the Works as the case may be. The Contractor shall allow and shall in no way hinder or delay the taking of the aforesaid measures. The Employer may deduct the reasonable cost of taking such measures from any monies due or to become due to the Contractor under this Contract (including any amount due under an agreement to which clause 27·5·2·1, or under an interim arrangement to which clause 27·5·3, refers) or may recover the same from the Contractor as a debt.

Consequences of determination under clauses 27·2 to 27·4

27·6   In the event of the determination of the employment of the Contractor under clause 27·2·2, 27·2·3, 27·3·3, 27·3·4 or 27·4 and so long as that employment has not been reinstated then:

27·6   ·1   the Employer may employ and pay other persons to carry out and complete the Works and to make good defects of the kind referred to in clause 17 and he or they may enter upon the site and the Works and use all temporary buildings, plant, tools, equipment and Site Materials, and may purchase all materials and goods necessary for the carrying out and completion of the Works and for the making good of defects as aforesaid; provided that where the aforesaid temporary buildings, plant, tools, equipment and Site Materials are not owned by the Contractor the consent of the owner thereof to such use is obtained by the Employer;

27·6   ·2 ·1   except where an insolvency event listed in clause 27·3·1 (other than the Contractor being a company making a proposal for a voluntary arrangement for a composition of debts or scheme of arrangement to be approved in accordance with the Companies Act 1985 or the insolvency Act 1986 as the case may be or any amendment or re-enactment) has occurred the Contractor shall, if so required by the Employer or by the Architect on behalf of the Employer within 14 days of the date of determination, assign to the Employer without payment the benefit of any agreement for the supply of materials or goods and/or for the execution of any work for the purposes of this Contract to the extent that the same is assignable;

    ·2 ·2   except where the Contractor has a trustee in bankruptcy appointed or being a company has a provisional liquidator appointed or has a petition alleging insolvency filed against it which is subsisting or passes a resolution for voluntary winding-up (other than for the purposes of amalgamation or reconstruction) which takes effect as a creditors' voluntary liquidation, the Employer may pay any supplier or sub-contractor for any materials or goods delivered or works executed for the purposes of this Contract before or after the date of determination in so far as the price thereof has not already been paid by the Contractor. Payments made under clause 27·6·2·2 may be deducted from any sum due or to become due to the Contractor or may be recoverable from the Contractor by the Employer as a debt;

27·6   ·3   the Contractor shall, when required in writing by the Architect so to do (but not before), remove from the Works any temporary buildings, plant, tools, equipment, goods and materials belonging to him and the Contractor shall have removed by their owner any temporary buildings, plant, tools, equipment, goods and materials not owned by him.

27·6 ·3 *continued*

If within a reasonable time after such requirement has been made the Contractor has not complied therewith in respect of temporary buildings, plant, tools, equipment, goods and materials belonging to him, then the Employer may (but without being responsible for any loss or damage) remove and sell any such property of the Contractor, holding the proceeds less all costs incurred to the credit of the Contractor.

27·6 ·4 ·1 Subject to clauses 27·5·3 and 27·6·4·2 the provisions of this Contract which require any further payment or any release or further release of Retention to the Contractor shall not apply; provided that clause 27·6·4·1 shall not be construed so as to prevent the enforcement by the Contractor of any rights under this Contract in respect of amounts properly due to be paid by the Employer to the Contractor which the Employer has unreasonably not paid and which, where clause 27·3·4 applies, have accrued 28 days or more before the date when under clause 27·3·4 the Employer could first give notice to determine the employment of the Contractor or, where clause 27·3·4 does not apply, which have accrued 28 days or more before the date of determination of the employment of the Contractor.

·4 ·2 Upon the completion of the Works and the making good of defects as referred to in clause 27·6·1 (but subject, where relevant, to the exercise of the right under clause 17·2 and/or clause 17·3 of the Architect, with the consent of the Employer, not to require defects of the kind referred to in clause 17 to be made good) then within a reasonable time thereafter an account in respect of the matters referred to in clause 27·6·5 shall be set out either in a statement prepared by the Employer or in a certificate issued by the Architect.

27·6 ·5 ·1 The amount of expenses properly incurred by the Employer including those incurred pursuant to clause 27·6·1 and of any direct loss and/or damage caused to the Employer as a result of the determination;

·5 ·2 the amount of any payment made to the Contractor;

·5 ·3 the total amount which would have been payable for the Works in accordance with this Contract.

27·6 ·6 If the sum of the amounts stated under clauses 27·6·5·1 and 27·6·5·2 exceeds or is less than the amount stated under clause 27·6·5·3 the difference shall be a debt payable by the Contractor to the Employer or by the Employer to the Contractor as the case may be.

Employer decides not to complete the Works

27·7 ·1 If the Employer decides after the determination of the employment of the Contractor not to have the Works carried out and completed, he shall so notify the Contractor in writing within 6 months from the date of such determination. Within a reasonable time from the date of such written notification the Employer shall send to the Contractor a statement of account setting out:

·1 ·1 the total value of work properly executed at the date of determination of the employment of the Contractor, such value to be ascertained in accordance with the Conditions as if the employment of the Contractor had not been determined, together with any amounts due to the Contractor under the Conditions not included in such total value;

·1 ·2 the amount of any expenses properly incurred by the Employer and of any direct loss and/or damage caused to the Employer as a result of the determination.

After taking into account amounts previously paid to the Contractor under this Contract, if the amount stated under clause 27·7·1·2 exceeds or is less than the amount stated under clause 27·7·1·1 the difference shall be a debt payable by the Contractor to the Employer or by the Employer to the Contractor as the case may be.

27·7 ·2 If after the expiry of the 6 month period referred to in clause 27·7·1 the Employer has not begun to operate the provisions of clause 27·6·1 and has not given a written notification pursuant to clause 27·7·1 the Contractor may require by notice in writing to the Employer that he states whether clauses 27·6·1 to 27·6·6 are to apply and, if not to apply, require that a statement of account pursuant to clause 27·7·1 be prepared by the Employer for submission to the Contractor.

Other rights and remedies

27·8 The provisions of clauses 27·2 to 27·7 are without prejudice to any other rights and remedies which the Employer may possess.

28 Determination by Contractor

Notices under clause 28

28·1 Any notice or further notice to which clauses 28·2·1, 28·2·2, 28·2·3, 28·2·4 and 28·3 refer shall be in writing and given by actual delivery or by special delivery or recorded delivery. If sent by special delivery or recorded delivery the notice or further notice shall, subject to proof to the contrary, be deemed to have been received 48 hours after the date of posting (excluding Saturday and Sunday and Public Holidays).

Default by Employer – suspension of uncompleted works

28·2 ·1 If the Employer shall make default in any one or more of the following respects:

·1 ·1 he does not pay by the final date for payment the amount properly due to the Contractor in respect of any certificate and/or any VAT on that amount pursuant to the VAT Agreement; or

·1 ·2 he interferes with or obstructs the issue of any certificate due under this Contract; or

·1 ·3 he fails to comply with the provisions of clause 19·1·1; or

·1 ·4 he fails pursuant to the Conditions to comply with the requirements of the CDM Regulations,

the Contractor may give to the Employer a notice specifying the default or defaults (the 'specified default or defaults').

28·2 ·2 If, before the date of Practical Completion, the carrying out of the whole or substantially the whole of the uncompleted Works is suspended for the continuous period of the length stated in the Appendix by reason of one or more of the following events:

·2 ·1 ·1 where an Information Release Schedule has been provided, failure of the Architect to comply with clause 5·4·1, or

·1 ·2 failure of the Architect to comply with clause 5·4·2, or

·2 ·2 Architect's instructions issued under clause 2·3, 13·2 or 23·2 unless caused by reason of some negligence or default of the Contractor, his servants or agents or of any person employed or engaged upon or in connection with the Works or any part thereof, his servants or agents other than a Nominated Sub-Contractor, the Employer or any person employed or engaged by the Employer; or

·2 ·3 delay in the execution of work not forming part of this Contract by the Employer himself or by persons employed or otherwise engaged by the Employer as referred to in clause 29 or the failure to execute such work or delay in the supply by the Employer of materials and goods which the Employer has agreed to supply for the Works or the failure so to supply; or

·2 ·4 failure of the Employer to give in due time ingress to or egress from the site of the Works or any part thereof through or over any land, buildings, way or passage adjoining or connected with the site and in the possession and control of the Employer, in accordance with the relevant Contract Documents, after receipt by the Architect of such notice, if any, as the Contractor is required to give, or failure of the Employer to give such ingress or egress as otherwise agreed between the Architect and the Contractor,

the Contractor may give to the Employer a notice specifying the event or events ('the specified suspension event or events').

28·2 ·3 If

– the Employer continues a specified default, or

– a specified suspension event is continued

for 14 days from receipt of the notice under clause 28·2·1 or clause 28·2·2 then the Contractor may on, or within 10 days from, the expiry of that 14 days by a further notice to the Employer determine the employment of the Contractor under this Contract. Such determination shall take effect on the date of receipt of such further notice.

28·2 ·4 If

- the Employer ends the specified default or defaults, or
- the specified suspension event or events cease, or
- the Contractor does not give the further notice referred to in clause 28·2·3

and

- the Employer repeats (whether previously repeated or not) a specified default, or
- a specified suspension event is repeated for whatever period (whether previously repeated or not), whereby the regular progress of the Works is or is likely to be materially affected

then, upon or within a reasonable time after such repetition, the Contractor may by notice to the Employer determine the employment of the Contractor under this Contract. Such determination shall take effect on the date of receipt of such notice.

28·2 ·5 A notice of determination under clause 28·2·3 or clause 28·2·4 shall not be given unreasonably or vexatiously.

Insolvency of Employer

28·3 ·1 If the Employer [II]

makes a composition or arrangement with his creditors, or becomes bankrupt, or,

being a company,

makes a proposal for a voluntary arrangement for a composition of debts or scheme of arrangement to be approved in accordance with the Companies Act 1985 or the Insolvency Act 1986 as the case may be or any amendment or re-enactment thereof, or

has a provisional liquidator appointed, or

has a winding-up order made, or

passes a resolution for voluntary winding-up (except for the purposes of amalgamation or reconstruction), or

under the Insolvency Act 1986 or any amendment or re-enactment thereof has an administrator or an administrative receiver appointed

then:

28·3 ·2 the Employer shall immediately inform the Contractor in writing if he has made a composition or arrangement with his creditors, or, being a company, has made a proposal for a voluntary arrangement for a composition of debts or scheme of arrangement to be approved in accordance with the Companies Act 1985 or the Insolvency Act 1986 or any amendment or re-enactment thereof as the case may be;

28·3 ·3 the Contractor may by notice to the Employer determine the employment of the Contractor under this Contract. Such determination shall take effect on the date of receipt of such notice. Provided that after the occurrence of any of the events set out in clause 28·3·1 and before the taking effect of any notice of determination of his employment issued by the Contractor pursuant to clause 28·3·3 the obligation of the Contractor to carry out and complete the Works in compliance with clause 2·1 shall be suspended.

Consequences of determination under clause 28·2 or 28·3

28·4 In the event of the determination of the employment of the Contractor under clause 28·2·3, 28·2·4 or 28·3·3 and so long as that employment has not been reinstated the provisions of clauses 28·4·1, 28·4·2 and 28·4·3 shall apply; such application shall be without prejudice to the accrued rights or remedies of either party or to any liability of the classes mentioned in clause 20 which may accrue either before the Contractor or any sub-contractors, their servants or agents or others employed on or engaged upon or in connection with the Works

---

Footnote   [II] See JCT Practice Note 24: after certain insolvency events an Insolvency Practitioner acts for the Employer.

28·4 *continued*

or any part thereof other than the Employer or any person employed or engaged by the Employer shall have removed his or their temporary buildings, plant, tools, equipment, goods or materials (including Site Materials) or by reason of his or their so removing the same. Subject to clauses 28·4·2 and 28·4·3 the provisions of this Contract which require any payment or release or further release of Retention to the Contractor shall not apply.

28·4 ·1 The Contractor shall, with all reasonable dispatch and in such manner and with such precautions as will prevent injury, death or damage of the classes in respect of which before the date of determination he was liable to indemnify the Employer under clause 20, remove from the site all his temporary buildings, plant, tools, equipment, goods and materials (including Site Materials) and shall ensure that his sub-contractors do the same, but subject always to the provisions of clause 28·4·3·5.

28·4 ·2 Within 28 days of the determination of the employment of the Contractor the Employer shall pay to the Contractor the Retention deducted by the Employer prior to the determination of the employment of the Contractor but subject to any right of the Employer of deduction therefrom which has accrued before the date of determination of the Contractor's employment.

28·4 ·3 The Contractor shall with reasonable dispatch prepare an account setting out the sum of the amounts referred to in clauses 28·4·3·1 to 28·4·3·5 which shall include as relevant amounts in respect of all Nominated Sub-Contractors:

·3 ·1 the total value of work properly executed at the date of determination of the employment of the Contractor, such value to be ascertained in accordance with the Conditions as if the employment of the Contractor had not been determined, together with any amounts due to the Contractor under the Conditions not included in such total value; and

·3 ·2 any sum ascertained in respect of direct loss and/or expense under clauses 26 and 34·3 (whether ascertained before or after the date of determination); and

·3 ·3 the reasonable cost of removal pursuant to clause 28·4·1; and

·3 ·4 any direct loss and/or damage caused to the Contractor by the determination; and

·3 ·5 the cost of materials or goods (including Site Materials) properly ordered for the Works for which the Contractor shall have paid or for which the Contractor is legally bound to pay, and on such payment in full by the Employer such materials or goods shall become the property of the Employer.

After taking into account amounts previously paid to the Contractor under this Contract the Employer shall pay to the Contractor the amount properly due in respect of this account within 28 days of its submission by the Contractor to the Employer but without any deduction of Retention.

Other rights and remedies

28·5 The provisions of clauses 28·2 to 28·4 are without prejudice to any other rights and remedies which the Contractor may possess.

28A Determination by Employer or Contractor

Grounds for determination of the employment of the Contractor

28A·1 ·1 If, before the date of Practical Completion, the carrying out of the whole or substantially the whole of the uncompleted Works is suspended for the relevant continuous period of the length stated in the Appendix by reason of one or more of the following events:

·1 ·1 force majeure; or

·1 ·2 loss or damage to the Works occasioned by any one or more of the Specified Perils; or

·1 ·3 civil commotion; or

·1 ·4 Architect's instructions issued under clause 2·3, 13·2 or 23·2 which have been issued as a result of the negligence or default of any local authority or statutory undertaker executing work solely in pursuance of its statutory obligations; or

28A·1 ·1 ·5 hostilities involving the United Kingdom (whether war be declared or not); or

·1 ·6 terrorist activity

then the Employer or the Contractor may upon the expiry of the aforesaid relevant period of suspension give notice in writing to the other by actual delivery or by special delivery or recorded delivery that unless the suspension is terminated within 7 days after the date of receipt of that notice the employment of the Contractor under this Contract will determine 7 days after the date of receipt of the aforesaid notice; and the employment of the Contractor shall so determine 7 days after receipt of such notice. If sent by special delivery or recorded delivery the notice shall, subject to proof to the contrary, be deemed to have been received 48 hours after the date of posting (excluding Saturday and Sunday and Public Holidays).

28A·1 ·2 The Contractor shall not be entitled to give notice under clause 28A·1·1 in respect of the matter referred to in clause 28A·1·1·2 where the loss or damage to the Works occasioned by any one or more of the Specified Perils was caused by some negligence or default of the Contractor, his servants or agents or of any person employed or engaged upon or in connection with the Works or any part thereof, his servants or agents other than the Employer or any person employed or engaged by the Employer or by any local authority or statutory undertaker executing work solely in pursuance of its statutory obligations.

28A·1 ·3 A notice of determination under clause 28A·1·1 shall not be given unreasonably or vexatiously.

Consequences of determination under clause 28A·1·1 – clauses 28A·3 to 28A·6

28A·2 Upon determination of the employment of the Contractor under clause 28A·1·1 the provisions of this Contract which require any further payment or any release or further release of Retention to the Contractor shall not apply; and the provisions of clauses 28A·3 to 28A·6 shall apply.

28A·3 The Contractor shall, with all reasonable dispatch and in such manner and with such precautions as will prevent injury, death or damage of the classes in respect of which before the date of determination of his employment he was liable to indemnify the Employer under clause 20, remove from the site all his temporary buildings, plant, tools, equipment, goods and materials (including Site Materials) and shall ensure that his sub-contractors do the same, but subject always to the provisions of clause 28A·5·4.

28A·4 The Employer shall pay to the Contractor one half of the Retention deducted by the Employer prior to the determination of the employment of the Contractor within 28 days of the date of determination of the Contractor's employment and the other half as part of the account to which clause 28A·5 refers but subject to any right of deduction therefrom which has accrued before the date of such determination.

28A·5 The Contractor shall, not later than 2 months after the date of the determination of the Contractor's employment, provide the Employer with all documents (including those relating to Nominated Sub-Contractors and Nominated Suppliers) necessary for the preparation of the account to which this clause refers. Subject to due discharge by the Contractor of this obligation the Employer shall with reasonable dispatch prepare an account setting out the sum of the amounts referred to in clauses 28A·5·1 to 28A·5·4 and, if clause 28A·6 applies, clause 28A·5·5, which shall include as relevant amounts in respect of all Nominated Sub-Contractors:

28A·5 ·1 the total value of work properly executed at the date of determination of the employment of the Contractor, such value to be ascertained in accordance with the Conditions as if the employment of the Contractor had not been determined, together with any amounts due to the Contractor under the Conditions not included in such total value; and

28A·5 ·2 any sum ascertained in respect of direct loss and/or expense under clauses 26 and 34·3 (whether ascertained before or after the date of determination); and

28A·5 ·3 the reasonable cost of removal under clause 28A·3; and

28A·5 ·4 the cost of materials or goods (including Site Materials) properly ordered for the Works for which the Contractor shall have paid or for which the Contractor is legally bound to pay, and on such payment in full by the Employer such materials or goods shall become the property of the Employer; and

28A·5 ·5 any direct loss and/or damage caused to the Contractor by the determination.

After taking into account amounts previously paid to the Contractor under this Contract the Employer shall pay to the Contractor the amount properly due in respect of this account within 28 days of its submission by the Employer to the Contractor but without deduction of any Retention.

28A·6 Where determination of the employment of the Contractor has occurred in respect of the matter referred to in clause 28A·1·1·2 and the loss or damage to the Works occasioned by any one or more of the Specified Perils was caused by some negligence or default of the Employer or of any person for whom the Employer is responsible, then upon such determination of the employment of the Contractor the account prepared under clause 28A·5 shall include the amount, if any, to which clause 28A·5·5 refers.

Amounts attributable to any Nominated Sub-Contractor

28A·7 The Employer shall inform the Contractor in writing which part or parts of the amounts paid or payable under clause 28A·5 is or are fairly and reasonably attributable to any Nominated Sub-Contractor and shall so inform each Nominated Sub-Contractor in writing.

29 Works by Employer or persons employed or engaged by Employer

Information in Contract Bills

29·1 Where the Contract Bills, in regard to any work not forming part of this Contract and which is to be carried out by the Employer himself or by persons employed or otherwise engaged by him, provide such information as is necessary to enable the Contractor to carry out and complete the Works in accordance with the Conditions, the Contractor shall permit the execution of such work.

Information not in Contract Bills

29·2 Where the Contract Bills do not provide the information referred to in clause 29·1 and the Employer requires the execution of work not forming part of this Contract by the Employer himself or by persons employed or otherwise engaged by the Employer, then the Employer may, with the consent of the Contractor (which consent shall not be unreasonably delayed or withheld), arrange for the execution of such work.

29·3 Every person employed or otherwise engaged by the Employer as referred to in clauses 29·1 and 29·2 shall for the purpose of clause 20 be deemed to be a person for whom the Employer is responsible and not to be a sub-contractor.

30 Certificates and payments

Payments subject to clause 31

30A Where it is stated in the Appendix that the Employer is a 'contractor' for the purposes of the Construction Industry Scheme or if at any time up to the payment of the Final Certificate the Employer becomes such a 'contractor' the obligation of the Employer to make any payment under or pursuant to this Contract is subject to clause 31.

Interim Certificates and valuations – final date for payment – interest

30·1 ·1 ·1 The Architect shall from time to time as provided in clause 30 issue Interim Certificates stating the amount due to the Contractor from the Employer specifying to what the amount relates and the basis on which that amount was calculated; and the final date for payment pursuant to an Interim Certificate shall be 14 days from the date of issue of each Interim Certificate.

If the Employer fails properly to pay the amount, or any part thereof, due to the Contractor under the Conditions by the final date for its payment the Employer shall pay to the Contractor in addition to the amount not properly paid simple interest thereon for the period until such payment is made. Payment of such simple interest shall be treated as a debt due to the Contractor by the Employer. The rate of interest payable shall be five per cent (5%) over the Base Rate of the Bank of England which is current at the date the payment by the Employer became overdue. Any payment of simple interest under this clause 30·1·1·1 shall not in any circumstances be construed as a waiver by the Contractor of his right to proper payment of the principal amount due from the Employer to the Contractor in accordance with, and within the time stated in, the Conditions or of the rights of the Contractor in regard to suspension of the performance of his obligations under this Contract to the Employer pursuant to clause 30·1·4 or to determination of his employment pursuant to the default referred to in clause 28·2·1·1.

30·1 ·1 ·2 Notwithstanding the fiduciary interest of the Employer in the Retention as stated in clause 30·5·1 the Employer is entitled to exercise any right under this Contract of withholding and/or deduction from monies due or to become due to the Contractor against any amount so due under an Interim Certificate whether or not any Retention is included in that Interim Certificate by the operation of clause 30·4. Such withholding and/or deduction is subject to the restriction in clause 35·13·5·3·2.

·1 ·3 Not later than 5 days after the date of issue of an Interim Certificate the Employer shall give a written notice to the Contractor which shall, in respect of the amount stated as due in that Interim Certificate, specify the amount of the payment proposed to be made, to what the amount of the payment relates and the basis on which that amount is calculated.

·1 ·4 Not later than 5 days before the final date for payment of the amount due pursuant to clause 30·1·1·1 the Employer may give a written notice to the Contractor which shall specify any amount proposed to be withheld and/or deducted from that due amount, the ground or grounds for such withholding and/or deduction and the amount of withholding and/or deduction attributable to each ground.

·1 ·5 Where the Employer does not give any written notice pursuant to clause 30·1·1·3 and/or to clause 30·1·1·4 the Employer shall pay the Contractor the amount due pursuant to clause 30·1·1·1.

Advance payment **30·1** ·1 ·6 Where it is stated in the Appendix that clause 30·1·1·6 applies, the advance payment identified in the Appendix shall be paid to the Contractor on the date stated in the Appendix and such advance payment shall be reimbursed to the Employer by the Contractor on the terms stated in the Appendix. Provided that where the Appendix states that an advance payment bond is required such payment shall only be made if the Contractor has provided to the Employer such bond from a surety approved by the Employer on the terms agreed between the British Bankers' Association and the JCT and annexed to the Appendix unless pursuant to the Seventh Recital a bond on other terms is required by the Employer.

Interim valuations **30·1** ·2 ·1 Interim valuations shall be made by the Quantity Surveyor whenever the Architect considers them to be necessary for the purpose of ascertaining the amount to be stated as due in an Interim Certificate. [mm]

Application by Contractor – amount of gross valuation

·2 ·2 Without prejudice to the obligation of the Architect to issue Interim Certificates as stated in clause 30·1·1·1, the Contractor, not later than 7 days before the date of an Interim Certificate, may submit to the Quantity Surveyor an application which sets out what the Contractor considers to be the amount of the gross valuation pursuant to clause 30·2. The Contractor shall include with his application any application made to the Contractor by a Nominated Sub-Contractor which sets out what the Nominated Sub-Contractor considers to be the amount of the gross valuation pursuant to clause 4·17 of Conditions NSC/C. If the Contractor submits such an application the Quantity Surveyor shall make an interim valuation. To the extent that the Quantity Surveyor disagrees with the gross valuation in the Contractor's application and/or in a Nominated Sub-Contractor's application the Quantity Surveyor at the same time as making the valuation shall submit to the Contractor a statement, which shall be in similar detail to that given in the application, which identifies such disagreement.

Issue of Interim Certificates **30·1** ·3 Interim Certificates shall be issued on the dates provided for in the Appendix and which dates shall continue up to the date of Practical Completion or to within one month thereafter. Thereafter Interim Certificates shall be issued as and when further amounts are ascertained as payable to the Contractor from the Employer and after the expiration of the Defects Liability Period named in the Appendix or upon the issue of the Certificate of Completion of Making Good Defects (whichever is the later) provided always that the Architect shall not be required to issue an Interim Certificate within one calendar month of having issued a previous Interim Certificate.

Footnote [mm] Where formula adjustment under clause 40 applies, clause 40·2·1 provides: 'Interim valuations shall be made before the issue of each Interim Certificate and accordingly the words "whenever the Architect considers them to be necessary" shall be deemed to have been deleted in clause 30·1·2·1.'

Right of suspension of obligations by Contractor

30·1 ·4 Without prejudice to any other rights and remedies which the Contractor may possess, if the Employer shall, subject to any notice issued pursuant to clause 30·1·1·4, fail to pay the Contractor in full (including any VAT due pursuant to the VAT Agreement) by the final date for payment as required by the Conditions and such failure shall continue for 7 days after the Contractor has given to the Employer, with a copy to the Architect, written notice of his intention to suspend the performance of his obligations under this Contract to the Employer and the ground or grounds on which it is intended to suspend performance then the Contractor may suspend such performance of his obligations under this Contract to the Employer until payment in full occurs. Such suspension shall not be treated as a suspension to which clause 27·2·1·1 refers or a failure to proceed regularly and diligently with the Works to which clause 27·2·1·2 refers.

Ascertainment of amounts due in Interim Certificates

30·2 The amount stated as due in an Interim Certificate, subject to any agreement between the parties as to stage payments, shall be the gross valuation as referred to in clause 30·2 less

any amount which may be deducted and retained by the Employer as provided in clause 30·4 (in the Conditions called 'the Retention') [mm·1] and

the total amount of any advance payment due for reimbursement to the Employer in accordance with the terms for such reimbursement stated in the Appendix pursuant to clause 30·1·1·6 and

the total amount of any advance payment due for reimbursement to the Employer in accordance with the terms of such reimbursement stated in NSC/T Part 1 pursuant to clause 4·1·2 of Conditions NSC/C and

the total amount stated as due in Interim Certificates previously issued under the Conditions.

The gross valuation shall be the total of the amounts referred to in clauses 30·2·1 and 30·2·2 less the total of the amounts referred to in clause 30·2·3 and applied up to and including a date not more than 7 days before the date of the Interim Certificate.

30·2 ·1 There shall be included the following which are subject to Retention:

·1 ·1 the total value of the work properly executed by the Contractor including any work so executed to which Alternative B in clause 13·4·1·2 applies or to which a Price Statement or any part thereof accepted pursuant to clause 13·4·1·2 paragraph A2 or amended Price Statement or any part thereof accepted pursuant to clause 13·4·1·2 paragraph A4·2 applies but excluding any restoration, replacement or repair of loss or damage and removal and disposal of debris which in clauses 22B·3·5 and 22C·4·4·2 are treated as if they were a Variation, together with, where applicable, any adjustment of that value under clause 40. Where it is stated in the Appendix that a priced Activity Schedule is attached thereto the value of the work to which the Activity Schedule relates shall be the total of the various sums which result from the application of the proportion of the work in an activity listed in the Activity Schedule properly executed to the price for that work as stated in the Activity Schedule;

·1 ·2 the total value of the materials and goods delivered to or adjacent to the Works for incorporation therein by the Contractor but not so incorporated, provided that the value of such materials and goods shall only be included as and from such times as they are reasonably, properly and not prematurely so delivered and are adequately protected against weather and other casualties;

·1 ·3 the total value of any materials or goods or items pre-fabricated which are 'listed items' the value of which is required pursuant to clause 30·3 to be included in the amount stated as due in the Interim Certificate;

·1 ·4 the amounts referred to in clause 4·17·1 of Conditions NSC/C in respect of each Nominated Sub-Contractor;

·1 ·5 the profit of the Contractor upon the total of the amounts referred to in clauses 30·2·1·4 and 30·2·2·5 less the total of the amount referred to in clause 30·2·3·2 at the rates included in the Contract Bills, or, in the case where the nomination arises from an instruction as to the expenditure of a provisional sum, at rates related thereto, or, if none, at reasonable rates.

Footnote

[mm·1] Optional clause 30·4A provides for a standard bond to be given in lieu of Retention. The terms of the bond are set out in Annex 3 to the Conditions. An entry should be made in the Appendix to state whether or not this optional clause applies.

30·2 ·2 There shall be included the following which are not subject to Retention:

    ·2 ·1 any amounts to be included in Interim Certificates in accordance with clause 3 as a result of payments made or costs incurred by the Contractor under clauses 6·2, 8·3, 9·2, 21·2·3, 22B·2 and 22C·3;

    ·2 ·2 any amounts ascertained under clause 26·1 or 34·3 or in respect of any restoration, replacement or repair of loss or damage and removal and disposal of debris which in clauses 22B·3·5 and 22C·4·4·2 are treated as if they were a Variation;

    ·2 ·3 any amount to which clause 35·17 refers;

    ·2 ·4 any amount payable to the Contractor under clause 38 or 39, if applicable;

    ·2 ·5 the amounts referred to in clause 4·17·2 of Conditions NSC/C in respect of each Nominated Sub-Contractor.

30·2 ·3 There shall be deducted the following which are not subject to Retention:

    ·3 ·1 any amount deductible under clause 7 or 8·4·2 or 17·2 or 17·3 or any amount allowable by the Contractor to the Employer under clause 38 or 39, if applicable;

    ·3 ·2 any amount referred to in clause 4·17·3 of Conditions NSC/C in respect of each Nominated Sub-Contractor.

Off-site materials or goods – 'the listed items'

30·3 The materials or goods or items pre-fabricated for inclusion in the Works to which this clause refers ('the listed items') shall have been listed by the Employer in a list supplied to the Contractor and annexed to the Contract Bills. The amount stated as due in an Interim Certificate shall include the value of any listed items before delivery thereof to or adjacent to the Works provided that the following conditions have been fulfilled:

30·3 ·1 the Contractor has provided the Architect with reasonable proof that the property in uniquely identified listed items is vested in the Contractor so that, pursuant to clause 16·2, after the amount in respect thereof included in an Interim Certificate as properly due to the Contractor has been paid by the Employer, the uniquely identified listed items shall become the property of the Employer; and, if so stated in the Appendix, has also provided from a surety approved by the Employer a bond in favour of the Employer on the terms agreed between the JCT and the British Bankers' Association and annexed to the Appendix unless pursuant to the Seventh recital a bond on other terms is required by the Employer;

30·3 ·2 the Contractor in respect of listed items which are not uniquely identified has provided the Architect

    with reasonable proof that the property in such listed items is vested in the Contractor so that, pursuant to clause 16·2, after the amount in respect thereof included in an Interim Certificate as properly due to the Contractor has been paid by the Employer, such listed items shall become the property of the Employer; and

    the Contractor has provided from a surety approved by the Employer a bond in favour of the Employer on the terms agreed between the JCT and the British Bankers' Association and annexed to the Appendix unless pursuant to the Seventh recital a bond on other terms is required by the Employer;

30·3 ·3 the listed items are in accordance with this Contract;

30·3 ·4 the listed items at the premises where they have been manufactured or assembled or stored

    either

    are set apart

    or

    have been clearly and visibly marked individually or in sets by letters or figures or by reference to a pre-determined code

    and identify

30·3 ·4 ·1 the Employer and to whose order they are held; and

·4 ·2 their destination as the Works;

30·3 ·5 the Contractor has provided the Employer with reasonable proof that the listed items are insured against loss or damage for their full value under a policy of insurance protecting the interests of the Employer and the Contractor in respect of the Specified Perils, during the period commencing with the transfer of property in the listed items to the Contractor until they are delivered to, or adjacent to, the Works.

Retention – rules for ascertainment

30·4 ·1 The Retention which the Employer may deduct and retain as referred to in clause 30·2 shall be such percentage of the total amount included under clause 30·2·1 in any Interim Certificate as arises from the operation of the following rules:

·1 ·1 the percentage (in the Conditions and Appendix called 'the Retention Percentage') deductible under clause 30·4·1·2 shall be 5 per cent (unless a lower rate shall have been agreed between the parties and specified in the Appendix as the Retention Percentage); and the percentage deductible under clause 30·4·1·3 shall be one half of the Retention Percentage; [nn]

·1 ·2 [oo] the Retention Percentage may be deducted from so much of the said total amount as relates to:

work which has not reached Practical Completion (as referred to in clauses 17·1, 18·1·1 or 35·16); and

amounts in respect of the value of materials and goods included under clauses 30·2·1·2, 30·2·1·3 and 30·2·1·4 (so far as that clause relates to materials and goods as referred to in clause 4·17·1 of Conditions NSC/C);

·1 ·3 [oo] half the Retention Percentage may be deducted from so much of the said total amount as relates to work which has reached Practical Completion (as referred to in clauses 17·1, 18·1·1 or 35·16) but in respect of which a Certificate of Completion of Making Good Defects under clause 17·4 or a certificate under clause 18·1·2 or an Interim Certificate under clause 35·17 has not been issued.

30·4 ·2 The Retention deducted from the value of work executed by the Contractor or any Nominated Sub-Contractor, and from the value of materials and goods intended for incorporation in the Works but not so incorporated, and specified in the statements issued under clause 30·5·2·1, is hereinafter referred to as the 'Contractor's retention' and the 'Nominated Sub-Contract retention' respectively.

Contractor's bond in lieu of Retention

30·4A ·1 Where it is stated in the Appendix that clause 30·4A applies, the provisions in clauses 30·2·1 and 30·4 which provide that the Employer may deduct and retain a percentage of the total amount included under clause 30·2·1 in any Interim Certificate ('the Retention') and in clause 30·5 *(Rules on treatment of Retention)* shall not apply; save that the Architect shall at the date of each Interim Certificate prepare, or instruct the Quantity Surveyor to prepare, a statement specifying what deduction in respect of the Contractor's Retention and of the Nominated Sub-Contract Retention for each Nominated Sub-Contractor would have been made, using the percentage stated in the Appendix pursuant to clause 30·4·1·1, in arriving at the amount stated as due in such Interim Certificate had the provisions in clauses 30·2·1 and 30·4 applied. [oo·1]

30·4A ·2 On or before the Date of Possession the Contractor shall provide and thereafter maintain a bond in favour of the Employer in the terms set out at **Annex 3** to the Conditions; and incorporating in clause 2 *(maximum aggregate sum)* and in clause 6(iii) *(expiry date)* of the bond, the sum and date stated in the Appendix. The bond executed by the surety named in the bond ('the Surety') shall be supplied to the Employer.

Footnotes

[nn] Where the Employer at the tender stage estimates the Contract Sum to be £500,000 or over, the Retention Percentage should not be more than 3 per cent.

[oo] By the operation of clauses 30·4·1·2 and 30·4·1·3 the Contractor will have released to him by the Employer upon payment of the next Interim Certificate after Practical Completion of the whole or part of the Works approximately one half of the Retention on the whole or the appropriate part; and upon payment of the next Interim Certificate after the expiration of the Defects Liability Period named in the Appendix, or after the issue of the Certificate of Completion of Making Good Defects, whichever is the later, the balance of the Retention on the whole or the appropriate part. When Retention is so included in Interim Certificates it becomes a 'sum due' to the Contractor and therefore subject to the rights of the Employer to deduct therefrom in accordance with the rights of the Employer so to deduct as set out in the Conditions.

[oo·1] This saving provision is included in view of the provisions in clauses 4(ii) and 4(iii) of the 'Bond in lieu of Retention' at Annex 3.

30·4A ·3 If the Contractor is in breach of clause 30·4A·2 by not providing and maintaining the bond the provisions of clauses 30·2·1, 30·4 and 30·5 which refer to the deduction and treatment of the Retention shall apply in respect of the next Interim Certificate and subsequent Interim Certificates issued after the date of the breach at the percentage stated in the Appendix pursuant to clause 30·4·1·1. If later the Contractor provides and thereafter maintains the required bond the Employer shall, in the next Interim Certificate after such compliance, have released to the Contractor and to any Nominated Sub-Contractor the Retention deducted during the period of the breach.

30·4A ·4 If at any time the Retention that would have been deducted had the provisions of clauses 30·2·1 and 30·4 applied exceeds the amount of the aggregate sum stated in the bond, then **either** the Contractor shall arrange with the Surety for the aggregate sum to equate to such Retention **or** the amount of such Retention not covered by the bond may be deducted by the Employer at the percentage stated in the Appendix pursuant to clause 30·4·1·1, and clauses 30·2, 30·4 and 30·5 shall apply to such Retention.

30·4A ·5 Where the Employer has required the Contractor to provide a Performance Bond, then, in respect of any default to which that Performance Bond refers which is also a matter for which the Employer could make a demand under the terms of the bond in lieu of Retention, the Employer shall first have recourse to the bond in lieu of Retention.

Rules on treatment of Retention

30·5 The Retention shall be subject to the following rules:

30·5 ·1 the Employer's interest in the Retention is fiduciary as trustee for the Contractor and for any Nominated Sub-Contractor (but without obligation to invest);

30·5 ·2 ·1 at the date of each Interim Certificate the Architect shall prepare, or instruct the Quantity Surveyor to prepare, a statement specifying the Contractor's retention and the Nominated Sub-Contract retention for each Nominated Sub-Contractor deducted in arriving at the amount stated as due in such Interim Certificate;

·2 ·2 such statement shall be issued by the Architect to the Employer, to the Contractor and to each Nominated Sub-Contractor whose work is referred to in the statement.

30·5 ·3 The Employer shall, to the extent that the Employer exercises his right under clause 30·4, if the Contractor or any Nominated Sub-Contractor so requests, at the date of payment under each Interim Certificate place the Retention in a separate banking account (so designated as to identify the amount as the Retention held by the Employer on trust as provided in clause 30·5·1) and certify to the Architect with a copy to the Contractor that such amount has been so placed. The Employer shall be entitled to the full beneficial interest in any interest accruing in the separate banking account and shall be under no duty to account for any such interest to the Contractor or any sub-contractor.

30·5 ·4 Where the Employer exercises the right to withhold and/or deduct referred to in clause 30·1·1·2 against any Retention he shall inform the Contractor of the amount of that withholding and/or deduction from either the Contractor's retention or the Nominated Sub-Contract retention of any Nominated Sub-Contractor by reference to the latest statement issued under clause 30·5·2·1.

Final adjustment of Contract Sum – documents from Contractor

30·6 ·1 ·1 Not later than 6 months after Practical Completion of the Works the Contractor shall provide the Architect, or, if so instructed by the Architect, the Quantity Surveyor, with all documents necessary for the purposes of the adjustment of the Contract Sum including all documents relating to the accounts of Nominated Sub-Contractors and Nominated Suppliers.

·1 ·2 Not later than 3 months after receipt by the Architect or by the Quantity Surveyor of the documents referred to in clause 30·6·1·1

·2 ·1 the Architect, or, if the Architect has so instructed, the Quantity Surveyor, shall ascertain (unless previously ascertained) any loss and/or expense under clauses 26·1, 26·4·1 and 34·3, and

·2 ·2 the Quantity Surveyor shall prepare a statement of all adjustments to be made to the Contract Sum as referred to in clause 30·6·2 other than any to which clause 30·6·1·2·1 applies

and the Architect shall forthwith send a copy of any ascertainment to which clause 30·6·1·2·1 refers and of the statement prepared in compliance with clause 30·6·1·2·2 to the Contractor and the relevant extract therefrom to each Nominated Sub-Contractor.

Items included in adjustment of Contract Sum

30·6 ·2 The Contract Sum shall be adjusted by:

- the amount of any Valuations agreed by the Employer and the Contractor to which clause 13·4·1·1 refers, and

- the amounts stated in any 13A Quotations for which the Architect has issued to the Contractor a confirmed acceptance pursuant to clause 13A·3·2 and for the amount of any Variations thereto as valued pursuant to clause 13A·8, and

- the amount of any Price Statement or any part thereof accepted pursuant to clause 13·4·1·2 paragraph A2 or amended Price Statement or any part thereof accepted pursuant to clause 13·4·1·2 paragraph A4·2

and as follows:

there shall be deducted:

·2 ·1 all prime cost sums, all amounts in respect of sub-contractors named as referred to in clause 35·1, the certified value of any work by a Nominated Sub-Contractor, whose employment has been determined in accordance with clause 35·24, which was not in accordance with the relevant Sub-Contract but which has been paid by the Employer, and any Contractor's profit thereon included in the Contract Bills;

·2 ·2 all provisional sums and the value of all work for which an Approximate Quantity is included in the Contract Bills;

·2 ·3 the amount of the valuation under clause 13·5·2 of items omitted in accordance with a Variation required by the Architect under clause 13·2, or subsequently sanctioned by him in writing, together with the amount included in the Contract Bills for any other work as referred to in clause 13·5·5 which is to be valued under clause 13·5;

·2 ·4 any amount deducted or deductible under clause 7 or 8·4·2 or 17·2 or 17·3 or any amount allowed or allowable to the Employer under clause 38, 39 or 40, whichever is applicable;

·2 ·5 any other amount which is required by this Contract to be deducted from the Contract Sum;

there shall be added:

·2 ·6 the amounts of the nominated sub-contract sums or tender sums for all Nominated Sub-Contractors as finally adjusted or ascertained under all relevant provisions of Conditions NSC/C;

·2 ·7 the tender sum (or such other sum as is appropriate in accordance with the terms of the tender as accepted by or on behalf of the Employer) for any work for which a tender made under clause 35·2 has been accepted;

·2 ·8 any amounts properly chargeable to the Employer in accordance with the nomination instruction of the Architect in respect of materials or goods supplied by Nominated Suppliers; such amounts shall include the discount for cash of 5 per cent referred to in clause 36 but shall exclude any value added tax which is treated, or is capable of being treated, as input tax by the Contractor;

·2 ·9 the profit of the Contractor upon the amounts referred to in clauses 30·6·2·6, 30·6·2·7 and 30·6·2·8 at the rates included in the Contract Bills or in the cases where the nomination arises from an instruction as to the expenditure of a provisional sum at rates related thereto or if none at reasonable rates;

·2 ·10 any amounts paid or payable by the Employer to the Contractor as a result of payments made or costs incurred by the Contractor under clauses 6·2, 8·3, 9·2 and 21·2·3;

·2 ·11 the amount of the Valuation under clause 13·5 of any Variation, including the valuation of other work as referred to in clause 13·5·5, other than the amount of the valuation of any omission under clause 13·5·2;

30·6 ·2 ·12 the amount of the Valuation of work executed by, or the amount of any disbursements by, the Contractor in accordance with instructions of the Architect as to the expenditure of provisional sums included in the Contract Bills and of all work for which an Approximate Quantity is included in the Contract Bills;

·2 ·13 any amount ascertained under clause 26·1 or 34·3;

·2 ·14 any amount paid by the Contractor under clause 22B or clause 22C which the Contractor is entitled to have added to the Contract Sum;

·2 ·15 any amount paid or payable to the Contractor under clause 38, 39 or 40, whichever is applicable;

·2 ·16 any other amount which is required by this Contract to be added to the Contract Sum;

·2 ·17 any amount to be paid in lieu of any ascertainment under clause 26·1 accepted pursuant to clause 13·4·1·2 paragraph A7.

Interim Certificate – final adjustment or ascertainment of nominated sub-contract sums

30·7 So soon as is practicable but not less than 28 days before the date of issue of the Final Certificate referred to in clause 30·8 and notwithstanding that a period of one month may not have elapsed since the issue of the previous Interim Certificate, the Architect shall issue an Interim Certificate the gross valuation for which shall include the amounts of the sub-contract sums for all Nominated Sub-Contracts as finally adjusted or ascertained under all relevant provisions of Conditions NSC/C.

Issue of Final Certificate

30·8 ·1 The Architect shall issue the Final Certificate (and inform each Nominated Sub-Contractor of the date of its issue) not later than 2 months after whichever of the following occurs last:

the end of the Defects Liability Period;

the date of issue of the Certificate of Completion of Making Good Defects under clause 17·4;

the date on which the Architect sent a copy to the Contractor of any ascertainment to which clause 30·6·1·2·1 refers and of the statement prepared in compliance with clause 30·6·1·2·2.

The Final Certificate shall state:

·1 ·1 the sum of the amounts already stated as due in Interim Certificates plus the amount of any advance payment paid pursuant to clause 30·1·1·6, and

·1 ·2 the Contract Sum adjusted as necessary in accordance with clause 30·6·2, and

·1 ·3 to what the amount relates and the basis on which the statement in the Final Certificate has been calculated

and the difference (if any) between the two sums shall (without prejudice to the rights of the Contractor in respect of any Interim Certificates which have subject to any notice issued pursuant to clause 30·1·1·4 not been paid in full by the Employer by the final date for payment of such Certificate) be expressed in the said Certificate as a balance due to the Contractor from the Employer or to the Employer from the Contractor as the case may be.

30·8 ·2 Not later than 5 days after the date of issue of the Final Certificate the Employer shall give a written notice to the Contractor which shall, in respect of any balance stated as due to the Contractor from the Employer in the Final Certificate, specify the amount of the payment proposed to be made, to what the amount of the payment relates and the basis on which that amount is calculated.

30·8 ·3 The final date for payment of the said balance payable by the Employer to the Contractor or by the Contractor to the Employer as the case may be shall be 28 days from the date of issue of the said Certificate. Not later than 5 days before the final date for payment of the balance the Employer may give a written notice to the Contractor which shall specify any amount proposed to be withheld and/or deducted from any balance due to the Contractor, the ground or grounds for such withholding and/or deduction and the amount of withholding and/or deduction attributable to each ground.

30·8 ·4 Where the Employer does not give a written notice pursuant to clause 30·8·2 and/or clause 30·8·3 the Employer shall pay the Contractor the balance stated as due to the Contractor in the Final Certificate.

30·8 ·5 If the Employer or the Contractor fails properly to pay the said balance, or any part thereof, by the final date for its payment the Employer or the Contractor as the case may be shall pay to the other, in addition to the balance not properly paid, simple interest thereon for the period until such payment is made. The rate of interest payable shall be five per cent (5%) over the Base Rate of the Bank of England which is current at the date the payment by the Employer or by the Contractor as the case may be became overdue. Any payment of simple interest under this clause 30·8 shall not in any circumstances be construed as a waiver by the Contractor or by the Employer as the case may be of his right to proper payment of the aforesaid balance due from the Employer to the Contractor or from the Contractor to the Employer in accordance with this clause 30·8.

30·8 ·6 Liability for payment of the balance pursuant to clause 30·8·3 and of any interest pursuant to clause 30·8·5 shall be treated as a debt due to the Contractor by the Employer or to the Employer by the Contractor as the case may be.

Effect of Final Certificate

30·9 ·1 Except as provided in clauses 30·9·2 and 30·9·3 (and save in respect of fraud), the Final Certificate shall have effect in any proceedings under or arising out of or in connection with this Contract (whether by adjudication under article 5 or by arbitration under article 7A or by legal proceedings under article 7B) as

·1 ·1 conclusive evidence that where and to the extent that any of the particular qualities of any materials or goods or any particular standard of an item of workmanship was described expressly in the Contract Drawings or the Contract Bills, or in any of the Numbered Documents, or in any instruction issued by the Architect under the Conditions, or in any drawings or documents issued by the Architect under clause 5·3·1·1 or 5·4 or 7, to be for the approval of the Architect, the particular quality or standard was to the reasonable satisfaction of the Architect, but such Certificate shall not be conclusive evidence that such or any other materials or goods or workmanship comply or complies with any other requirement or term of this Contract, and

·1 ·2 conclusive evidence that any necessary effect has been given to all the terms of this Contract which require that an amount is to be added to or deducted from the Contract Sum or an adjustment is to be made of the Contract Sum save where there has been any accidental inclusion or exclusion of any work, materials, goods or figure in any computation or any arithmetical error in any computation, in which event the Final Certificate shall have effect as conclusive evidence as to all other computations, and

·1 ·3 conclusive evidence that all and only such extensions of time, if any, as are due under clause 25 have been given, and

·1 ·4 conclusive evidence that the reimbursement of direct loss and/or expense, if any, to the Contractor pursuant to clause 26·1 is in final settlement of all and any claims which the Contractor has or may have arising out of the occurrence of any of the matters referred to in clause 26·2 whether such claim be for breach of contract, duty of care, statutory duty or otherwise.

30·9 ·2 If any adjudication, arbitration or other proceedings have been commenced by either Party before the Final Certificate has been issued the Final Certificate shall have effect as conclusive evidence as provided in clause 30·9·1 after either

·2 ·1 such proceedings have been concluded, whereupon the Final Certificate shall be subject to the terms of any decision, award or judgment in or settlement of such proceedings, or

·2 ·2 a period of 12 months after the issue of the Final Certificate during which neither Party has taken any further step in such proceedings, whereupon the Final Certificate shall be subject to any terms agreed in partial settlement,

whichever shall be the earlier.

30·9 ·3 If any adjudication, arbitration or other proceedings have been commenced by either Party within 28 days after the Final Certificate has been issued, the Final Certificate shall have effect as conclusive evidence as provided in clause 30·9·1 save only in respect of all matters to which those proceedings relate.

30·9 ·4 Where pursuant to clause 41A·7·1 either Party wishes to have a dispute or difference on which an Adjudicator has given his decision on a date which is after the date of issue of the Final Certificate finally determined by arbitration or legal proceedings, either Party may commence arbitration or legal proceedings within 28 days of the date on which the Adjudicator gave his decision.

Effect of certificates other than Final Certificate

30·10 Save as aforesaid no certificate of the Architect shall of itself be conclusive evidence that

30·10 ·1 any works, materials or goods

or

30·10 ·2 any Performance Specified Work

to which it relates are in accordance with this Contract.

31 Construction Industry Scheme (CIS)

Definitions

31·1 In this clause and in the Appendix:

'the Act' means the Income and Corporation Taxes Act 1988 or any statutory amendment or modification thereof;

'Authorisation' means:

either 'CIS 4', the registration card designated 'CIS 4(T)' and which has an expiry date or 'CIS 4(P)', in the form provided by regulations 7 and 7C of the Regulations appearing as shown in Schedule 1 of the Regulations and issued by the Inland Revenue;

or 'CIS 5' or 'CIS 6', the certificates in the form provided by regulation 24 of the Regulations and appearing as shown in Schedule 1 of the Regulations and issued by the Inland Revenue;

or a 'certifying document' created on the Contractor's letter headed stationery, not a fax or photocopy, in the form prescribed by regulation 34 of the Regulations;

'construction operations' means those operations defined in S.567 of the Act as construction operations;

'contractor' means a person who is a contractor for the purposes of the Act and the Regulations;

'the direct cost of materials' means the direct cost to the Contractor or to any other person of materials used or to be used in carrying out the construction operations to which the contract under which the payment is made relates as provided in regulation 7 of the Regulations;

'the Regulations' means the Income Tax (Sub-Contractors in the Construction Industry) Regulations 1993 S.I. No. 743 as amended by the Income Tax (Sub-Contractors in the Construction Industry) (Amendment) Regulations 1998 S.I. No. 2622 or any amendment or re-making thereof;

'statutory deduction' means the deduction which is in force at the time of payment referred to in S.559(4) and (4A) of the Act;

'sub-contractor' means a person who is a sub-contractor for the purposes of the Act and the Regulations;

'voucher' means:

either a tax payment voucher in the form CIS 25 provided by regulation 7 and appearing as shown in Schedule 1 of the Regulations and issued by the Inland Revenue;

or a gross payment voucher CIS 24 in the form provided by regulation 29 and appearing as shown in Schedule 1 of the Regulations and issued by the Inland Revenue.

Whether Employer is a 'contractor'

31·2 Where it is stated in the Appendix that the Employer is not a 'contractor' clauses 31·3 to 31·14 shall not apply. Nevertheless if, at any time up to the payment of the Final Certificate, the Employer becomes such a 'contractor', the Employer shall so inform the Contractor and the provisions of clauses 31·3 to 31·14 shall thereupon become operative.

Payment by Employer – valid Authorisation essential

31·3 The Employer shall not make any payment under or pursuant to this Contract unless a valid Authorisation has been provided to him or his nominated representative by the Contractor.

Validity of Authorisation – Employer's query

31·4 ·1 If the Employer or his nominated representative is not satisfied with the validity of the Authorisation provided by the Contractor, he shall thereupon notify the Contractor in writing of his grounds for considering that the Authorisation is not valid.

31·4 ·2 Where a notification has been given under clause 31·4·1, the Employer shall not make any payment under or pursuant to this Contract until

    either   the Employer or his nominated representative has received an Authorisation which he considers to be valid

    or   the Contractor has re-submitted the Authorisation with a letter from the Contractor's tax office, confirming that that Authorisation is valid.

Authorisation: CIS 4 registration card

31·5 ·1 Where the Authorisation is a CIS 4 registration card, then 7 days before the final date for payment of any sum due:

    ·1 ·1 the Contractor shall give to the Employer a statement showing the direct cost of materials to the Contractor and to any other persons to be included in the payment; and

    ·1 ·2 the Employer shall make the statutory deduction from that part of the payment which is not in respect of the direct cost of materials as stated by the Contractor pursuant to clause 31·5·1·1.

31·5 ·2 Where the Contractor complies with clause 31·5·1·1 he shall indemnify the Employer against any loss or expense caused to the Employer by any incorrect statement of the amount of direct cost referred to in clause 31·5·1·1.

31·5 ·3 Where the Contractor fails to comply with clause 31·5·1·1, or where the Employer has reasonable grounds to believe that any statement provided in compliance with clause 31·5·1·1 is incorrect, the Employer shall make a fair estimate of the direct cost of materials.

Authorisation: CIS 5 or CIS 6 or a certifying document

31·6 Where the Authorisation is a valid CIS 5 or CIS 6 or a certifying document the Employer shall pay any amount due without making the statutory deduction.

Change of Authorisation

31·7 Where the Authorisation is a CIS 4 but the Contractor is subsequently issued with a CIS 5 or CIS 6 by the Inland Revenue, the Contractor shall immediately inform the Employer and either present the CIS 5 or CIS 6 in person to the Employer or his nominated representative or send to the Employer or his nominated representative a certifying document. Provided the Employer or his nominated representative is satisfied with the validity of the changed Authorisation, clause 31·6 shall thereupon apply.

31·8 If an Authorisation CIS 5 or CIS 6 is withdrawn by the Inland Revenue for any reason, the Contractor shall thereupon notify the Employer or his authorised representative and the Employer shall make no further payments to the Contractor under or pursuant to this Contract until the Contractor provides the Employer or his authorised representative with a valid Authorisation CIS 4. After such provision clauses 31·5·1, 31·5·2 and 31·5·3 shall apply.

31·9 If an Authorisation CIS 5 or CIS 6 expires, the Employer shall make no further payments to the Contractor under or pursuant to this Contract until the Contractor:

    either   shows in person to the Employer or his nominated representative an Authorisation CIS 4 and if so clauses 31·5·1, 31·5·2 and 31·5·3 shall apply;

    or   provides to the Employer or his nominated representative an Authorisation CIS 5 or CIS 6 or a certifying document and if so clause 31·6 shall apply.

Vouchers	31·10	Where Authorisation CIS 4 applies and the Employer has made payments to the Contractor, the Employer shall within 14 days of the end of the income tax month [oo·2] in which the payment is made provide the Contractor with a copy of the CIS 25 voucher that he has sent to the Inland Revenue showing all the payments made in the tax month concerned and the total tax deducted.
	31·11	Where Authorisation CIS 6 applies and the Employer has made payments to the Contractor, the Contractor shall within 14 days of the end of the income tax month [oo·2] in which the payment is made provide the CIS 24 voucher to the Employer who shall add thereto his tax reference and send the voucher to the Inland Revenue with a copy to the Contractor.
Correction of errors in making the statutory deduction	31·12	Where the Employer has made an error or omission in calculating the statutory deduction, he may correct the error by repayment or further deduction from payments due to the Contractor, subject only to an instruction by the Inland Revenue to the Employer not to make such a correction.
Relation to other clauses	31·13	If compliance with this clause 31 involves the Employer or the Contractor in not complying with any other of the Conditions, then the provisions of this clause shall prevail.
Disputes or differences	31·14	The relevant procedures applicable under this Contract to the resolution of disputes or differences between the Employer and the Contractor shall apply to any dispute or difference between the Employer and the Contractor as to the operation of this clause 31 except where the Act or the Regulations or any other Act of Parliament or statutory instrument, rule or order made under any Act of Parliament provide for some other method of resolving such dispute or difference.
	32	[Number not used]
	33	[Number not used]

34 Antiquities

Effect of find of antiquities	34·1	All fossils, antiquities and other objects of interest or value which may be found on the site or in excavating the same during the progress of the Works shall become the property of the Employer and upon discovery of such an object the Contractor shall forthwith:
	34·1 ·1	use his best endeavours not to disturb the object and shall cease work if and insofar as the continuance of work would endanger the object or prevent or impede its excavation or its removal;
	34·1 ·2	take all steps which may be necessary to preserve the object in the exact position and condition in which it was found; and
	34·1 ·3	inform the Architect or the clerk of works of the discovery and precise location of the object.
Architect's instructions on antiquities found	34·2	The Architect shall issue instructions in regard to what is to be done concerning an object reported by the Contractor under clause 34·1, and (without prejudice to the generality of his power) such instructions may require the Contractor to permit the examination, excavation or removal of the object by a third party. Any such third party shall for the purposes of clause 20 be deemed to be a person for whom the Employer is responsible and not to be a sub-contractor.
Direct loss and/or expense	34·3 ·1	If in the opinion of the Architect compliance with the provisions of clause 34·1 or with an instruction issued under clause 34·2 has involved the Contractor in direct loss and/or expense for which he would not be reimbursed by a payment made under any other provision of this Contract then the Architect himself shall ascertain or shall instruct the Quantity Surveyor to ascertain the amount of such loss and/or expense.
	34·3 ·2	If and to the extent that it is necessary for the ascertainment of such loss and/or expense the Architect shall state in writing to the Contractor what extension of time, if any, has been made under clause 25 in respect of the Relevant Event referred to in clause 25·4·5·1 so far as that clause refers to clause 34.
	34·3 ·3	Any amount from time to time so ascertained shall be added to the Contract Sum.

Footnote [oo·2] The income tax month ends on the 5th day of the month.

Part 2: Nominated Sub-Contractors and Nominated Suppliers

Nominated Sub-Contractors

35 GENERAL

Definition of a Nominated Sub-Contractor

35·1 Where

35·1 ·1 in the Contract Bills; or

35·1 ·2 in any instruction of the Architect under clause 13·3 on the expenditure of a provisional sum included in the Contract Bills; or

35·1 ·3 in any instruction of the Architect under clause 13·2 requiring a Variation to the extent, but not further or otherwise,

·3 ·1 that it consists of work additional to that shown upon the Contract Drawings and described by or referred to in the Contract Bills and

·3 ·2 that any supply and fixing of materials or goods or any execution of work by a Nominated Sub-Contractor in connection with such additional work is of a similar kind to any supply and fixing of materials or the execution of work for which the Contract Bills provided that the Architect would nominate a sub-contractor; or

35·1 ·4 by agreement (which agreement shall not be unreasonably delayed or withheld) between the Contractor and the Architect on behalf of the Employer

the Architect has, whether by the use of a prime cost sum or by naming a sub-contractor, reserved to himself the final selection and approval of the sub-contractor to the Contractor who shall supply and fix any materials or goods or execute work, the sub-contractor so named or to be selected and approved shall be nominated in accordance with the provisions of clause 35 and a sub-contractor so nominated shall be a Nominated Sub-Contractor for all the purposes of this Contract. The provisions of clause 35·1 shall apply notwithstanding any requirement of the Standard Method of Measurement for a PC sum to be included in the Bills of Quantities in respect of Nominated Sub-Contractors.

Contractor's tender for works otherwise reserved for a Nominated Sub-Contractor

35·2 ·1 Where the Contractor in the ordinary course of his business directly carries out works included in the Contract Bills and to which clause 35 applies, and where items of such works are set out in the Appendix and the Architect is prepared to receive tenders from the Contractor for such items, then the Contractor shall be permitted to tender for the same or any of them but without prejudice to the Employer's right to reject the lowest or any tender. If the Contractor's tender is accepted, he shall not sub-let the work to a Domestic Sub-Contractor without the consent of the Architect. Provided that where an item for which the Architect intends to nominate a sub-contractor is included in Architect's instructions issued under clause 13·3 it shall be deemed for the purposes of clause 35·2·1 to have been included in the Contract Bills and the item of work to which it relates shall likewise be deemed to have been set out in the Appendix.

35·2 ·2 It shall be a condition of any tender accepted under clause 35·2 that clause 13 shall apply in respect of the items of work included in the tender as if for the reference therein to the Contract Drawings and the Contract Bills there were references to the equivalent documents included in or referred to in the tender submitted under clause 35·2.

35·2 ·3 None of the provisions of clause 35 other than clause 35·2 shall apply to works for which a tender of the Contractor is accepted under clause 35·2.

PROCEDURE FOR NOMINATION OF A SUB-CONTRACTOR

35·3 The nomination of a sub-contractor to which clause 35·1 applies shall be effected in accordance with clauses 35·4 to 35·9 inclusive.

Documents relating to Nominated Sub-Contractors

35·4 The following documents relating to Nominated Sub-Contractors are issued by the JCT and are referred to in the Conditions and in those documents by the use either of the name or of the identification term:

Name of document	*Identification term*
The Standard Form of Nominated Sub-Contract Tender 1998 Edition which comprises:	NSC/T
Part 1: The Employer's Invitation to Tender to a Sub-Contractor	– Part 1
Part 2: Tender by a Sub-Contractor	– Part 2
Part 3: Particular Conditions (to be agreed by a Contractor and a Sub-Contractor nominated under clause 35·6)	– Part 3
The Standard Form of Articles of Nominated Sub-Contract Agreement between a Contractor and a Nominated Sub-Contractor, 1998 Edition	Agreement NSC/A
The Standard Conditions of Nominated Sub-Contract, 1998 Edition, incorporated by reference into Agreement NSC/A	Conditions NSC/C
The Standard Form of Employer/Nominated Sub-Contractor Agreement, 1998 Edition	Agreement NSC/W
The Standard Form of Nomination Instruction for a Sub-Contractor	Nomination NSC/N

Contractor's right of reasonable objection

35·5 ·1 No person against whom the Contractor makes a reasonable objection shall be a Nominated Sub-Contractor. The Contractor shall make such reasonable objection in writing at the earliest practicable moment but in any case not later than 7 working days from receipt of the instruction of the Architect under clause 35·6 nominating the sub-contractor.

35·5 ·2 Where such reasonable objection is made the Architect may either issue further instructions to remove the objection so that the Contractor can then comply with clause 35·7 in respect of such nomination instruction or cancel such nomination instruction and issue an instruction either under clause 13·2 omitting the work which was the subject of that nomination instruction or under clause 35·6 nominating another sub-contractor therefor. A copy of any instruction issued under clause 35·5·2 shall be sent by the Architect to the sub-contractor.

Architect's instruction on Nomination NSC/N – documents accompanying the instruction

35·6 The Architect shall issue an instruction to the Contractor on Nomination NSC/N nominating the sub-contractor which shall be accompanied by:

35·6 ·1 NSC/T Part 1 completed by the Architect and NSC/T Part 2 completed and signed by the sub-contractor and signed by or on behalf of the Employer as 'approved' together with a copy of the numbered tender documents listed in and enclosed with NSC/T Part 1 together with any additional documents and/or amendments thereto as have been approved by the Architect;

35·6 ·2 a copy of the completed Agreement NSC/W entered into between the Employer and the sub-contractor;

35·6 ·3 confirmation of any alterations to the information given in NSC/T Part 1

item 7: obligations or restrictions imposed by the Employer
item 8: order of Works: Employer's requirements
item 9: type and location of access; and

35·6 ·4 a copy of the Principal Contractor's Health and Safety Plan.

– copy of instruction to sub-contractor

A copy of the instruction shall be sent by the Architect to the sub-contractor together with a copy of the completed Appendix for the Main Contract.

Contractor's obligations on receipt of Architect's instruction	**35·7**		The Contractor shall forthwith upon receipt of such instruction:
	35·7	·1	complete in agreement with the sub-contractor NSC/T Part 3 and have that completed NSC/T Part 3 signed by or on behalf of the Contractor and by or on behalf of the sub-contractor; and
	35·7	·2	execute Agreement NSC/A with the sub-contractor

and thereupon shall send a copy of the completed Agreement NSC/A and of the agreed and signed NSC/T Part 3 (but **not** the other Annexures to Agreement NSC/A) to the Architect.

Non-compliance with clause 35·7 – Contractor's obligation to notify Architect	**35·8**		If the Contractor, having used his best endeavours, has not, within 10 working days from receipt of such instruction, complied with clause 35·7, the Contractor shall thereupon by a notice in writing inform the Architect

either

	35·8	·1	of the date by which he expects to have complied with clause 35·7

or

	35·8	·2	that the non-compliance is due to other matters identified in the Contractor's notice. [pp]
Architect's duty on receipt of any notice under clause 35·8	**35·9**		Within a reasonable time after receipt of a notice under clause 35·8 the Architect shall:
	35·9	·1	where **clause 35·8·1 applies**, after consultation with the Contractor and so far as he considers it reasonable, fix a later date by which the Contractor shall have complied with clause 35·7;
	35·9	·2	where **clause 35·8·2 applies**, inform the Contractor in writing

> either that he does not consider that the matters identified in the notice justify non-compliance by the Contractor with such nomination instruction, in which case the Contractor shall comply with clause 35·7 in respect of such nomination instruction
>
> or that he does consider that the matters identified in the notice justify non-compliance by the Contractor with such nomination instruction, in which case the Architect shall either issue further instructions so that the Contractor can then comply with clause 35·7 in respect of such nomination instruction or cancel such nomination instruction and issue an instruction either under clause 13·2 omitting the work which was the subject of the nomination instruction or under clause 35·6 nominating another sub-contractor therefor. A copy of any instruction issued under clause 35·9·2 shall be sent by the Architect to the sub-contractor.

35·10 [Number not used]

35·11 [Number not used]

35·12 [Number not used]

Footnote

[pp] The "other matters identified in the Contractor's notice" may include: any discrepancy in or divergence between the numbered tender documents or a discrepancy in or divergence between the numbered tender documents and the documents referred to in clauses 2·3·1 to 2·3·4; and any reasons given to the Contractor by the sub-contractor for not agreeing the items in NSC/T Part 3 or for not being prepared to have NSC/T Part 3 signed by or on his behalf which may relate to: the items in the Main Contract Appendix sent to him by the Architect with a copy of the nomination instruction differing from those in the Main Contract Appendix attached to the Architect's Invitation to Tender (NSC/T Part 1); or to any information given to him in items 7, 8 and 9 of the Architect's Invitation to Tender having been changed as confirmed by the Architect when issuing his nomination instruction (see clause 35·6·3), which changes have to be identified in NSC/T Part 3.

PAYMENT OF NOMINATED SUB-CONTRACTOR

Architect – direction as to interim payment for Nominated Sub-Contractor

35·13 ·1 The Architect shall on the issue of each Interim Certificate:

·1 ·1 direct the Contractor as to the amount of each interim or final payment to Nominated Sub-Contractors which is included in the amount stated as due in Interim Certificates and the amount of such interim or final payment shall be computed by the Architect in accordance with the relevant provisions of Conditions NSC/C; and

·1 ·2 forthwith inform each Nominated Sub-Contractor of the amount of any interim or final payment directed in accordance with clause 35·13·1·1.

35·13 ·2 Each payment directed under clause 35·13·1·1 shall be paid by the Contractor by the final date for its payment in accordance with Conditions NSC/C.

Direct payment of Nominated Sub-Contractor

35·13 ·3 Before the issue of each Interim Certificate (other than the first Interim Certificate) and of the Final Certificate the Contractor shall provide the Architect with reasonable proof of payment by the Contractor pursuant to clause 35·13·2.

35·13 ·4 If the Contractor is unable to provide the reasonable proof referred to in clause 35·13·3 because of some failure or omission of the Nominated Sub-Contractor to provide any document or other evidence to the Contractor which the Contractor may reasonably require and the Architect is reasonably satisfied that this is the sole reason why reasonable proof is not furnished by the Contractor, the provisions of clause 35·13·5 shall not apply and the provisions of clause 35·13·3 shall be regarded as having been satisfied.

35·13 ·5 ·1 If the Contractor fails to provide reasonable proof under clause 35·13·3, the Architect shall issue a certificate to that effect stating the amount in respect of which the Contractor has failed to provide such proof, and the Architect shall issue a copy of the certificate to the Nominated Sub-Contractor concerned.

·5 ·2 Provided that the Architect has issued the certificate under clause 35·13·5·1, and subject to clause 35·13·5·3, the amount of any future payment otherwise due to the Contractor under this Contract (after deducting any amounts due to the Employer from the Contractor under this Contract) shall be reduced by any amounts due to Nominated Sub-Contractors which the Contractor has failed to pay (together with the amount of any value added tax which would have been due to the Nominated Sub-Contractors) and the Employer shall himself pay the same to the Nominated Sub-Contractors concerned. Provided that the Employer shall in no circumstances be obliged to pay amounts to Nominated Sub-Contractors in excess of amounts available for reduction as aforesaid.

·5 ·3 The operation of clause 35·13·5·2 shall be subject to the following:

·3 ·1 where the Contractor would otherwise be entitled to payment of an amount stated as due in an Interim Certificate under clause 30, the reduction and payment to the Nominated Sub-Contractors referred to in clause 35·13·5·2 shall be made at the same time as the Employer pays the Contractor any balance due under clause 30 or, if there is no such balance, not later than the expiry of the period of 14 days within which the Contractor would otherwise be entitled to payment;

·3 ·2 where the sum due to the Contractor is the Retention or any part thereof, the reduction and payment to the Nominated Sub-Contractors referred to in clause 35·13·5·2 shall not exceed any part of the Contractor's retention (as defined in clause 30·4·2) which would otherwise be due for payment to the Contractor;

·3 ·3 where the Employer has to pay 2 or more Nominated Sub-Contractors but the amount due or to become due to the Contractor is insufficient to enable the Employer to pay the Nominated Sub-Contractors in full, the Employer shall apply the amount available pro rata to the amounts from time to time remaining unpaid by the Contractor or adopt such other method of apportionment as may appear to the Employer to be fair and reasonable having regard to all the relevant circumstances;

35·13 ·5 *continued*

·3 ·4 clause 35·13·5·2 shall cease to have effect absolutely if at the date when the reduction and payment to the Nominated Sub-Contractors referred to in clause 35·13·5·2 would otherwise be made there is in existence

either a Petition which has been presented to the Court for the winding up of the Contractor

or a resolution properly passed for the winding up of the Contractor other than for the purposes of amalgamation or reconstruction

whichever shall have first occurred. [qq]

Agreement NSC/W – pre-nomination payments to Nominated Sub-Contractor by Employer

35·13 ·6 Where, in accordance with clause 2·2 of Agreement NSC/W, the Employer, before the date of the issue of an instruction nominating a sub-contractor, has paid to him an amount in respect of design work and/or materials or goods and/or fabrication which is/are included in the subject of the sub-contract sum or tender sum:

·6 ·1 the Employer shall send to the Contractor the written statement of the Nominated Sub-Contractor of the amount to be credited to the Contractor, and

·6 ·2 the Employer may make withholdings or deductions up to the amount of such credit from the amounts stated as due to the Contractor in any of the Interim Certificates which include amounts of interim or final payment to the Nominated Sub-Contractor; provided that the amount so withheld or deducted from that stated as due in any one Interim Certificate shall not exceed the amount of payment to the Nominated Sub-Contractor included therein as directed by the Architect.

EXTENSION OF PERIOD OR PERIODS FOR COMPLETION OF NOMINATED SUB-CONTRACT WORKS

35·14 ·1 The Contractor shall not grant to any Nominated Sub-Contractor any extension of the period or periods within which the sub-contract works (or where the sub-contract works are to be completed in parts any part thereof) are to be completed except in accordance with the relevant provisions of Conditions NSC/C which require the written consent of the Architect to any such grant.

35·14 ·2 The Architect shall operate the relevant provisions of Conditions NSC/C upon receiving any notice, particulars and estimate and a request from the Contractor and any Nominated Sub-Contractor for his written consent to an extension of the period or periods for the completion of the sub-contract works or any part thereof as referred to in clause 2·3 of Conditions NSC/C.

FAILURE TO COMPLETE NOMINATED SUB-CONTRACT WORKS

35·15 ·1 If any Nominated Sub-Contractor fails to complete the sub-contract works (or where the sub-contract works are to be completed in parts any part thereof) within the period specified in the Nominated Sub-Contract or within any extended time granted by the Contractor with the written consent of the Architect, and the Contractor so notifies the Architect with a copy to the Nominated Sub-Contractor, then, provided that the Architect is satisfied that clause 35·14 has been properly applied, the Architect shall so certify in writing to the Contractor. Immediately upon the issue of such a certificate the Architect shall send a duplicate thereof to the Nominated Sub-Contractor.

35·15 ·2 The certificate of the Architect under clause 35·15·1 shall be issued not later than 2 months from the date of notification to the Architect that the Nominated Sub-Contractor has failed to complete the sub-contract works or any part thereof.

Footnote

[qq] Where the Contractor is a person subject to bankruptcy laws and not the law relating to the insolvency of a company, clause 35·13·5·3·4 will require amendment to refer to the events on the happening of which bankruptcy occurs. (See also footnote [a].)

PRACTICAL COMPLETION OF NOMINATED SUB-CONTRACT WORKS

35·16 When in the opinion of the Architect practical completion of the works executed by a Nominated Sub-Contractor is achieved and the Sub-Contractor has complied sufficiently with clause 5E·2·5 of Conditions NSC/C he shall forthwith issue a certificate to that effect and practical completion of such works shall be deemed to have taken place on the day named in such certificate, a duplicate copy of which shall be sent by the Architect to the Nominated Sub-Contractor; where clause 18 applies practical completion of works executed by a Nominated Sub-Contractor in a relevant part shall be deemed to have occurred on the relevant date to which clause 18·1 refers and the Architect shall send to the Nominated Sub-Contractor a copy of the written statement which he has issued pursuant to clause 18·1.

EARLY FINAL PAYMENT OF NOMINATED SUB-CONTRACTORS

35·17 Provided clause 5 of Agreement NSC/W remains in force unamended, then at any time after the day named in the certificate issued under clause 35·16 the Architect may, and on the expiry of 12 months from the aforesaid day shall, issue an Interim Certificate the gross valuation for which shall include the amount of the relevant sub-contract sum or ascertained final sub-contract sum as finally adjusted or ascertained under the relevant provisions of Conditions NSC/C; provided always that the Nominated Sub-Contractor:

35·17 ·1 has in the opinion of the Architect and the Contractor remedied any defects, shrinkages or other faults which have appeared and which the Nominated Sub-Contractor is bound to remedy under the Nominated Sub-Contract; and

35·17 ·2 has sent through the Contractor to the Architect or the Quantity Surveyor all documents necessary for the final adjustment of the sub-contract sum or the computation of the ascertained final sub-contract sum referred to in clause 35·17.

Defects in nominated sub-contract works after final payment of Nominated Sub-Contractor – before issue of Final Certificate

35·18 Upon payment by the Contractor by the final date for payment to the Nominated Sub-Contractor ('the original sub-contractor') of the amount certified under clause 35·17 then:

35·18 ·1 ·1 if the original sub-contractor fails to rectify any defect, shrinkage or other fault in the sub-contract works which he is bound to remedy under the Nominated Sub-Contract and which appears before the issue of the Final Certificate under clause 30·8 the Architect shall issue an instruction nominating a person ('the substituted sub-contractor') to carry out such rectification work and all the provisions relating to Nominated Sub-Contractors in clause 35 shall apply to such further nomination;

·1 ·2 the Employer shall take such steps as may be reasonable to recover, under the Agreement NSC/W, from the original sub-contractor a sum equal to the sub-contract price of the substituted sub-contractor. The Contractor shall pay or allow to the Employer any difference between the amount so recovered by the Employer and the sub-contract price of the substituted sub-contractor provided that, before the further nomination has been made, the Contractor has agreed (which agreement shall not be unreasonably delayed or withheld) to the sub-contract price to be charged by the substituted sub-contractor.

35·18 ·2 Nothing in clause 35·18 shall override or modify the provisions of clause 35·21.

Final payment – saving provisions

35·19 Notwithstanding any final payment to a Nominated Sub-Contractor under the provisions of clause 35:

35·19 ·1 until the date of Practical Completion of the Works or the date when the Employer takes possession of the Works, whichever first occurs, the Contractor shall be responsible for loss or damage to the sub-contract works for which a payment to which clause 35·17 refers has been made to the same extent but not further or otherwise than he is responsible for that part of the Works for which a payment as aforesaid has not been made;

35·19 ·2 the provisions of clause 22A or 22B or 22C whichever is applicable shall remain in full force and effect.

POSITION OF EMPLOYER IN RELATION TO NOMINATED SUB-CONTRACTOR

35·20　Neither the existence nor the exercise of the powers in clause 35 nor anything else contained in the Conditions shall render the Employer in any way liable to any Nominated Sub-Contractor except by way and in the terms of the Agreement NSC/W.

CLAUSE 2·1 OF AGREEMENT NSC/W – POSITION OF CONTRACTOR

35·21　The Contractor shall not be responsible to the Employer for:

　·1　the design of any nominated sub-contract works insofar as such nominated sub-contract works have been designed by a Nominated Sub-Contractor;

　·2　the selection of the kinds of materials and goods for any nominated sub-contract works insofar as such kinds of materials and goods have been selected by a Nominated Sub-Contractor;

　·3　the satisfaction of any performance specification or requirement insofar as such performance specification or requirement is included or referred to in the description of any nominated sub-contract works included in or annexed to the numbered tender documents enclosed with any NSC/T Part 1;

　·4　the provision of any information required to be provided pursuant to Agreement NSC/W in reasonable time so that the Architect can comply with the provisions of clauses 5·4·1 and 5·4·2 in respect thereof.

Nothing in this clause 35·21 shall affect the obligations of the Contractor under this Contract in regard to the supply of workmanship, materials and goods by a Nominated Sub-Contractor.

RESTRICTIONS IN CONTRACTS OF SALE ETC. – LIMITATION OF LIABILITY OF NOMINATED SUB-CONTRACTORS

35·22　Where any liability of the Nominated Sub-Contractor to the Contractor is limited under the provisions of clause 1·7 of Conditions NSC/C, the liability of the Contractor to the Employer shall be limited to the same extent.

35·23　[Number not used]

CIRCUMSTANCES WHERE RE-NOMINATION NECESSARY

35·24　If in respect of any Nominated Sub-Contract:

35·24　·1　the Contractor informs the Architect that in the opinion of the Contractor the Nominated Sub-Contractor has made default in respect of any one or more of the matters referred to in clauses 7·1·1·1 to 7·1·1·4 of Conditions NSC/C; and the Contractor has passed to the Architect any observations of the Nominated Sub-Contractor in regard to the matters on which the Contractor considers the Nominated Sub-Contractor is in default; and the Architect is reasonably of the opinion that the Nominated Sub-Contractor has made default; or

35·24　·2　the Contractor informs the Architect that one of the insolvency events referred to in clause 7·2·1 of Conditions NSC/C *(Insolvency of Nominated Sub-Contractor)* has occurred and **either** that under clause 7·2·3 of the aforesaid Conditions the employment of the Nominated Sub-Contractor has been automatically determined **or** that under clause 7·2·4 of those Conditions the Contractor has an option, with the written consent of the Architect, to determine the employment of the Nominated Sub-Contractor; or

35·24　·3　the Nominated Sub-Contractor determines his employment under clause 7·7 of Conditions NSC/C; or

35·24 ·4 the Contractor has been required by the Employer to determine the employment of the Nominated Sub-Contractor under clause 7·3 of Conditions NSC/C and has so determined that employment; or

35·24 ·5 work properly executed or materials or goods properly fixed or supplied by the Nominated Sub-Contractor have to be taken down and/or re-executed or re-fixed or re-supplied ('work to be re-executed') as a result of compliance by the Contractor or by any other Nominated Sub-Contractor with any instruction or other exercise of a power of the Architect under clauses 7 or 8·4 or 17·2 or 17·3 and the Nominated Sub-Contractor cannot be required under the Nominated Sub-Contract and does not agree to carry out the work to be re-executed;

then:

35·24 ·6 Where **clause 35·24·1 applies**:

·6 ·1 the Architect shall issue an instruction to the Contractor to give to the Nominated Sub-Contractor the notice specifying the default or defaults to which clause 7·1·1 of Conditions NSC/C refers; and may in that instruction state that the Contractor must obtain a further instruction of the Architect before determining the employment of the Nominated Sub-Contractor under clause 7·1·2 or 7·1·3 of Conditions NSC/C; and

·6 ·2 the Contractor shall inform the Architect whether, following the giving of that notice for which the Architect has issued an instruction under clause 35·24·6·1, the employment of the Nominated Sub-Contractor has been determined by the Contractor under clause 7·1·2 or 7·1·3 of Conditions NSC/C; or where the further instruction referred to in clause 35·24·6·1 has been given by the Architect the Contractor shall confirm that the employment of the Nominated Sub-Contractor has been determined; then

·6 ·3 if the Contractor informs or confirms to the Architect that the employment of the Nominated Sub-Contractor has been so determined the Architect shall make such further nomination of a sub-contractor in accordance with clause 35 as may be necessary to supply and fix the materials or goods or to execute the work and to make good or re-supply or re-execute as necessary any work executed by or any materials or goods supplied by the Nominated Sub-Contractor whose employment has been determined which were not in accordance with the relevant Nominated Sub-Contract.

35·24 ·7 ·1 Where **clause 35·24·2 applies** and the Contractor has an option under clause 7·2·4 of Conditions NSC/C *(Insolvency of Nominated Sub-Contractor)* to determine the employment of the Nominated Sub-Contractor, clause 35·24·7·2 shall apply in respect of the written consent of the Architect to any determination of the employment of the Nominated Sub-Contractor.

·7 ·2 Where

– the administrator or the administrative receiver of the Nominated Sub-Contractor, or

– the Nominated Sub-Contractor after making a composition or arrangement with his creditors or, being a company, after making a voluntary arrangement for a composition of debts or a scheme of arrangement approved in accordance with the Companies Act 1985 or the Insolvency Act 1986 or any amendment or re-enactment thereof as the case may be

is, to the reasonable satisfaction of the Contractor and the Architect, prepared and able to continue to carry out the relevant Nominated Sub-Contract and to meet the liabilities thereunder, the Architect may withhold his consent. Where continuation on such terms does not apply the Architect shall give his consent to a determination by the Contractor of the employment of the Nominated Sub-Contractor unless the Employer and the Contractor otherwise agree.

·7 ·3 Where the written consent of the Architect to the determination of the employment of the Nominated Sub-Contractor has been given and the Contractor has determined that employment or where, under clause 7·2·3 of the Conditions NSC/C, the employment of the Nominated Sub-Contractor has been automatically determined the following shall apply. The Architect shall make such further nomination of a sub-contractor in accordance with clause 35 as may be necessary to supply and fix the materials or goods or to execute the work and to make good or re-

35·24 ·7 ·3 *continued*

supply or re-execute as necessary any work executed by or any materials or goods supplied by the Nominated Sub-Contractor whose employment has been determined which were not in accordance with the relevant Nominated Sub-Contract.

·7 ·4 Where **clause 35·24·4 applies** the Architect shall make such further nomination of a sub-contractor in accordance with clause 35 as may be necessary to supply and fix the materials or goods or to execute the work and to make good or re-supply or re-execute as necessary any work executed by or any materials or goods supplied by the Nominated Sub-Contractor whose employment has been determined which were not in accordance with the relevant Nominated Sub-Contract.

35·24 ·8 ·1 Where **clause 35·24·3 applies** the Architect shall make such further nomination of a sub-contractor in accordance with clause 35 as may be necessary to supply and fix the materials or goods or to execute the work and to make good or re-supply or re-execute as necessary any work executed by or any materials or goods supplied by the Nominated Sub-Contractor who has determined his employment which were not in accordance with the relevant Nominated Sub-Contract.

·8 ·2 Where **clause 35·24·5 applies** the Architect shall make such further nomination of a sub-contractor in accordance with clause 35 as may be necessary to carry out the work to be re-executed referred to in clause 35·24·5.

35·24 ·9 The amount properly payable to the Nominated Sub-Contractor under the Nominated Sub-Contract resulting from such further nomination under clause 35·24·6·3 or 35·24·7·3 or 35·24·7·4 shall be included in the amount stated as due in Interim Certificates and added to the Contract Sum. Where clauses 35·24·3 and 35·24·8·1 apply any extra amount, payable by the Employer in respect of the sub-contractor nominated under the further nomination over the price of the Nominated Sub-Contractor who has validly determined his employment under his Nominated Sub-Contract, and where clauses 35·24·5 and 35·24·8·2 apply the amount payable by the Employer, resulting from such further nomination may at the time or any time after such amount is certified in respect of the sub-contractor nominated under the further nomination be deducted by the Employer from monies due or to become due to the Contractor under this Contract or may be recoverable from the Contractor by the Employer as a debt.

35·24 ·10 The Architect shall make the further nomination of a sub-contractor as referred to in clauses 35·24·6·3, 35·24·7, 35·24·8·1 and 35·24·8·2 within a reasonable time, having regard to all the circumstances, after the obligation to make such further nomination has arisen.

DETERMINATION OR DETERMINATION OF EMPLOYMENT OF NOMINATED SUB-CONTRACTOR – ARCHITECT'S INSTRUCTIONS

35·25 The Contractor shall not determine any Nominated Sub-Contract by virtue of any right to which he may be or may become entitled without an instruction from the Architect so to do.

35·26 ·1 Where the employment of the Nominated Sub-Contractor is determined under clauses 7·1 to 7·5 of Conditions NSC/C, the Architect shall provide the Contractor with the information and with the direction in an Interim Certificate to enable the Contractor to comply with clause 7·5·2 of Conditions NSC/C: namely the amount of expenses properly incurred by the Employer and the amount of direct loss and/or damage caused to the Employer by the determination of the employment of the Nominated Sub-Contractor; and shall, pursuant to clause 35·13·1, issue an Interim Certificate which certifies the value of any work executed or goods and materials supplied by the Nominated Sub-Contractor to the extent that such value has not been included in previous Interim Certificates.

35·26 ·2 Where the employment of the Nominated Sub-Contractor is determined under clause 7·7 of Conditions NSC/C and clause 7·8 of those Conditions applies, the Architect shall, pursuant to clause 35·13·1, issue an Interim Certificate which certifies the value of any work executed or goods and materials supplied by the Nominated Sub-Contractor to the extent that such value has not been included in previous Interim Certificates.

Nominated Suppliers

Definition of a Nominated Supplier

36·1 ·1 In the Conditions 'Nominated Supplier' means a supplier to the Contractor who is nominated by the Architect in one of the following ways to supply materials or goods which are to be fixed by the Contractor:

·1 ·1 where a prime cost sum is included in the Contract Bills in respect of those materials or goods and the supplier is either named in the Contract Bills or subsequently named by the Architect in an instruction issued under clause 36·2;

·1 ·2 where a provisional sum is included in the Contract Bills and in any instruction by the Architect in regard to the expenditure of such sum the supply of materials or goods is made the subject of a prime cost sum and the supplier is named by the Architect in that instruction or in an instruction issued under clause 36·2;

·1 ·3 where a provisional sum is included in the Contract Bills and in any instruction by the Architect in regard to the expenditure of such a sum materials or goods are specified for which there is a sole source of supply in that there is only one supplier from whom the Contractor can obtain them, in which case the supply of materials or goods shall be made the subject of a prime cost sum in the instructions issued by the Architect in regard to the expenditure of the provisional sum and the sole supplier shall be deemed to have been nominated by the Architect;

·1 ·4 where the Architect requires under clause 13·2, or subsequently sanctions, a Variation and specifies materials or goods for which there is a sole supplier as referred to in clause 36·1·1·3, in which case the supply of the materials or goods shall be made the subject of a prime cost sum in the instruction or written sanction issued by the Architect under clause 13·2 and the sole supplier shall be deemed to have been nominated by the Architect.

36·1 ·2 In the Conditions the expression 'Nominated Supplier' shall not apply to a supplier of materials or goods which are specified in the Contract Bills to be fixed by the Contractor unless such materials or goods are the subject of a prime cost sum in the Contract Bills, notwithstanding that the supplier has been named in the Contract Bills or that there is a sole supplier of such materials or goods as defined in clause 36·1·1·3.

Architect's instructions

36·2 The Architect shall issue instructions for the purpose of nominating a supplier for any materials or goods in respect of which a prime cost sum is included in the Contract Bills or arises under clause 36·1.

Ascertainment of costs to be set against prime cost sum

36·3 ·1 For the purposes of clause 30·6·2·8 the amounts 'properly chargeable to the Employer in accordance with the nomination instruction of the Architect' shall include the total amount paid or payable in respect of the materials or goods less any discount other than the discount referred to in clause 36·4·4, properly so chargeable to the Employer and shall include where applicable:

·1 ·1 any tax (other than any value added tax which is treated, or is capable of being treated, as input tax by the Contractor) or duty not otherwise recoverable under this Contract by whomsoever payable which is payable under or by virtue of any Act of Parliament on the import, purchase, sale, appropriation, processing, alteration, adapting for sale or use of the materials or goods to be supplied; and

·1 ·2 the net cost of appropriate packing, carriage and delivery after allowing for any credit for return of any packing to the supplier; and

·1 ·3 the amount of any price adjustment properly paid or payable to, or allowed or allowable by, the supplier less any discount other than a cash discount for payment in full within 30 days of the end of the month during which delivery is made.

36·3 ·2 Where in the opinion of the Architect the Contractor properly incurs expense, which would not be reimbursed under clause 36·3·1 or otherwise under this Contract, in obtaining the materials or goods from the Nominated Supplier such expense shall be added to the Contract Sum.

Sale contract provisions – Architect's right to nominate supplier

36·4 Save where the Architect and the Contractor shall otherwise agree, the Architect shall only nominate as a supplier a person who will enter into a contract of sale with the Contractor which provides, inter alia:

36·4 ·1 that the materials or goods to be supplied shall be of the quality and standard specified provided that where and to the extent that approval of the quality of materials or of the standards of workmanship is a matter for the opinion of the Architect such quality and standards shall be to the reasonable satisfaction of the Architect;

36·4 ·2 that the Nominated Supplier shall make good by replacement or otherwise any defects in the materials or goods supplied which appear up to and including the last day of the Defects Liability Period under this Contract and shall bear any expenses reasonably incurred by the Contractor as a direct consequence of such defects provided that:

·2 ·1 where the materials or goods have been used or fixed such defects are not such that reasonable examination by the Contractor ought to have revealed them before using or fixing;

·2 ·2 such defects are due solely to defective workmanship or material in the materials or goods supplied and shall not have been caused by improper storage by the Contractor or by misuse or by any act or neglect of either the Contractor, the Architect or the Employer or by any person or persons for whom they may be responsible or by any other person for whom the Nominated Supplier is not responsible;

36·4 ·3 that delivery of the materials or goods supplied shall be commenced, carried out and completed in accordance with a delivery programme to be agreed between the Contractor and the Nominated Supplier including, to the extent agreed, the following grounds on which that programme may be varied:

force majeure; or

civil commotion, local combination of workmen, strike or lock-out; or

any instruction of the Architect under clause 13·2 *(Variations)* or clause 13·3 *(provisional sums)*; or

failure of the Architect to supply to the Nominated Supplier within due time any necessary information for which he has specifically applied in writing on a date which was neither unreasonably distant from nor unreasonably close to the date on which it was necessary for him to receive the same; or

exceptionally adverse weather conditions

or, if no such programme is agreed, delivery shall be commenced, carried out and completed in accordance with the reasonable directions of the Contractor;

36·4 ·4 that the Nominated Supplier shall allow the Contractor a discount for cash of 5 per cent on all payments if the Contractor makes payment in full within 30 days of the end of the month during which delivery is made;

36·4 ·5 that the Nominated Supplier shall not be obliged to make any delivery of materials or goods (except any which may have been paid for in full less only any discount for cash) after the determination (for any reason) of the Contractor's employment under this Contract;

36·4 ·6 that full discharge by the Contractor in respect of payments for materials or goods supplied by the Nominated Supplier shall be effected within 30 days of the end of the month during which delivery is made less only a discount for cash of 5 per cent if so paid;

36·4 ·7 that the ownership of materials or goods shall pass to the Contractor upon delivery by the Nominated Supplier to or to the order of the Contractor, whether or not payment has been made in full;

36·4 ·8 that if any dispute or difference between the Contractor and the Nominated Supplier is referred to arbitration the provisions of clause 41B shall apply;

36·4 ·9 that no provision in the contract of sale shall override, modify or affect in any way whatsoever the provisions in the contract of sale which are included therein to give effect to clauses 36·4·1 to 36·4·9 inclusive.

Contract of sale – restriction, limitation or exclusion of liability

36·5 ·1 Subject to clauses 36·5·2 and 36·5·3, where the said contract of sale between the Contractor and the Nominated Supplier in any way restricts, limits or excludes the liability of the Nominated Supplier to the Contractor in respect of materials or goods supplied or to be supplied, and the Architect has specifically approved in writing the said restrictions, limitations or exclusions, the liability of the Contractor to the Employer in respect of the said materials or goods shall be restricted, limited or excluded to the same extent.

36·5 ·2 The Contractor shall not be obliged to enter into a contract with the Nominated Supplier until the Architect has specifically approved in writing the said restrictions, limitations or exclusions.

36·5 ·3 Nothing in clause 36·5 shall be construed as enabling the Architect to nominate a supplier otherwise than in accordance with the provisions stated in clause 36·4.

Part 3: Fluctuations

Choice of fluctuation provisions – entry in Appendix

37 ·1 Fluctuations shall be dealt with in accordance with whichever of the following alternatives
clause 38; or
clause 39 [rr]; or
clause 40 [ss]
is identified in the Appendix. The provisions so identified shall be [tt] deemed to be incorporated with the Conditions as executed by the parties hereto.

37 ·2 Clause 38 shall apply where neither clause 39 nor clause 40 is identified in the Appendix.

37 ·3 Neither clause 38 nor clause 39 nor clause 40 shall apply in respect of the work for which the Architect has issued to the Contractor a confirmed acceptance of a 13A Quotation or in respect of a Variation to such work.

Clause 38: Contribution, levy and tax fluctuations
Clause 39: Labour and materials cost and tax fluctuations
Clause 40: Use of price adjustment formulae

These clauses are published separately in 'Fluctuations: Fluctuation clauses for use with the Private versions'.

Footnotes

[rr] Clause 39 should be used where the parties have agreed to allow the labour and materials cost and tax fluctuations to which clauses 39·1 to ·3 refer. Alternatively, clause 40 should be used where the parties have agreed that fluctuations shall be dealt with by adjustment of the Contract Sum under the Price Adjustment Formulae for Building Contracts.

[ss] Clause 40 is used where the parties have agreed that fluctuations shall be dealt with by adjustment of the Contract Sum under the Price Adjustment Formulae for Building Contracts.

[tt] Notwithstanding the provisions of clause 37·1 on deemed incorporation the parties may nevertheless wish to incorporate the agreed alternative fluctuation provisions in the executed Contract.

Part 4: Settlement of disputes – adjudication – arbitration – legal proceedings [uu]

41A Adjudication [uu·1]

Application of clause 41A

41A·1 Clause 41A applies where, pursuant to article 5, either Party refers any dispute or difference arising under this Contract to adjudication.

Identity of Adjudicator

41A·2 The Adjudicator to decide the dispute or difference shall be either an individual agreed by the Parties or, on the application of either Party, an individual to be nominated as the Adjudicator by the person named in the Appendix ('the nominator'). Provided that [vv]

41A·2 ·1 no Adjudicator shall be agreed or nominated under clause 41A·2 or clause 41A·3 who will not execute the Standard Agreement for the appointment of an Adjudicator issued by the JCT (the 'JCT Adjudication Agreement' [ww]) with the Parties, [vv] and

41A·2 ·2 where either Party has given notice of his intention to refer a dispute or difference to adjudication then

– any agreement by the Parties on the appointment of an adjudicator must be reached with the object of securing the appointment of, and the referral of the dispute or difference to, the Adjudicator within 7 days of the date of the notice of intention to refer *(see clause 41A·4·1)*;

– any application to the nominator must be made with the object of securing the appointment of, and the referral of the dispute or difference to, the Adjudicator within 7 days of the date of the notice of intention to refer.

Upon agreement by the Parties on the appointment of the Adjudicator or upon receipt by the Parties from the nominator of the name of the nominated Adjudicator the Parties shall thereupon execute with the Adjudicator the JCT Adjudication Agreement.

Death of Adjudicator – inability to adjudicate

41A·3 If the Adjudicator dies or becomes ill or is unavailable for some other cause and is thus unable to adjudicate on a dispute or difference referred to him, then either the Parties may agree upon an individual to replace the Adjudicator or either Party may apply to the nominator for the nomination of an adjudicator to adjudicate that dispute or difference; and the Parties shall execute the JCT Adjudication Agreement with the agreed or nominated Adjudicator.

Dispute or difference – notice of intention to refer to adjudication – referral

41A·4 ·1 When pursuant to article 5 a Party requires a dispute or difference to be referred to adjudication then that Party shall give notice to the other Party of his intention to refer the dispute or difference, briefly identified in the notice, to adjudication. If an Adjudicator is agreed or appointed within 7 days of the notice then the Party giving the notice shall refer the dispute or difference to the Adjudicator ('the referral') within 7 days of the notice. If an Adjudicator is not agreed or appointed within 7 days of the notice the referral shall be made immediately on such agreement or appointment. The said Party shall include with that referral particulars of the dispute or difference together with a summary of the contentions on which he relies, a statement of the relief or remedy which is sought and any material he wishes the Adjudicator to consider. The referral and its accompanying documentation shall be copied simultaneously to the other Party.

Footnotes

[uu] It is open to the Employer and the Contractor to resolve disputes by the process of Mediation: see Practice Note 28 'Mediation on a Building Contract or Sub-Contact Dispute'.

[uu·1] The time periods generally specified in this clause are those defined by stattute. Where the nature of the dispute or the work concerned may have any significant effect upon the progress or cost of the Works such as works relating to the primary structural elements the Adjudicator should consider an accelerated time table for the adjudication procedures: see JCT Practice Note 2 (Series 2): Adjudication under JCT Forms.

[vv] The nominators named in the Appendix have agreed with the JCT that they will comply with the requirements of clause 41A on the nomination of an adjudicator including the requirement in clause 41A·2·2 for the nomination to be made with the object of securing the appointment of, and the referral of the dispute or difference to, the Adjudicator within 7 days of the date of the notice of intention to refer; and will only nominate adjudicators who will enter into the 'JCT Adjudication Agreement'.

[ww] The JCT Adjudication Agreement is available from the retailers of JCT Forms.
A version of this Agreement is also available for use if the Parties have named an Adjudicator in their contract.

41A·4 ·2 The referral by a Party with its accompanying documentation to the Adjudicator and the copies thereof to be provided to the other Party shall be given by actual delivery or by FAX or by special delivery or recorded delivery. If given by FAX then, for record purposes, the referral and its accompanying documentation must forthwith be sent by first class post or given by actual delivery. If sent by special delivery or recorded delivery the referral and its accompanying documentation shall, subject to proof to the contrary, be deemed to have been received 48 hours after the date of posting subject to the exclusion of Sundays and any Public Holiday.

Conduct of the adjudication

41A·5 ·1 The Adjudicator shall immediately upon receipt of the referral and its accompanying documentation confirm the date of that receipt to the Parties.

41A·5 ·2 The Party not making the referral may, by the same means stated in clause 41A·4·2, send to the Adjudicator within 7 days of the date of the referral, with a copy to the other Party, a written statement of the contentions on which he relies and any material he wishes the Adjudicator to consider.

41A·5 ·3 The Adjudicator shall within 28 days of the referral under clause 41A·4·1 and acting as an Adjudicator for the purposes of S.108 of the Housing Grants, Construction and Regeneration Act 1996 and not as an expert or an arbitrator reach his decision and forthwith send that decision in writing to the Parties. Provided that the Party who has made the referral may consent to allowing the Adjudicator to extend the period of 28 days by up to 14 days; and that by agreement between the Parties after the referral has been made a longer period than 28 days may be notified jointly by the Parties to the Adjudicator within which to reach his decision.

41A·5 ·4 The Adjudicator shall not be obliged to give reasons for his decision.

41A·5 ·5 In reaching his decision the Adjudicator shall act impartially and set his own procedure; and at his absolute discretion may take the initiative in ascertaining the facts and the law as he considers necessary in respect of the referral which may include the following:

·5 ·1 using his own knowledge and/or experience;

·5 ·2 subject to clause 30·9, opening up, reviewing and revising any certificate, opinion, decision, requirement or notice issued, given or made under this Contract as if no such certificate, opinion, decision, requirement or notice had been issued, given or made;

·5 ·3 requiring from the Parties further information than that contained in the notice of referral and its accompanying documentation or in any written statement provided by the Parties including the results of any tests that have been made or of any opening up;

·5 ·4 requiring the Parties to carry out tests or additional tests or to open up work or further open up work;

·5 ·5 visiting the site of the Works or any workshop where work is being or has been prepared for this Contract;

·5 ·6 obtaining such information as he considers necessary from any employee or representative of the Parties provided that before obtaining information from an employee of a Party he has given prior notice to that Party;

·5 ·7 obtaining from others such information and advice as he considers necessary on technical and on legal matters subject to giving prior notice to the Parties together with a statement or estimate of the cost involved;

·5 ·8 having regard to any term of this Contract relating to the payment of interest, deciding the circumstances in which or the period for which a simple rate of interest shall be paid.

41A·5 ·6 Any failure by either Party to enter into the JCT Adjudication Agreement or to comply with any requirement of the Adjudicator under clause 41A·5·5 or with any provision in or requirement under clause 41A shall not invalidate the decision of the Adjudicator.

41A·5 ·7 The Parties shall meet their own costs of the adjudication except that the Adjudicator may direct as to who should pay the cost of any test or opening up if required pursuant to clause 41A·5·5·4.

41A·5 ·8 Where any dispute or difference arises under clause 8·4·4 as to whether an instruction issued thereunder is reasonable in all the circumstances the following provisions shall apply:

·8 ·1 The Adjudicator to decide such dispute or difference shall (where practicable) be an individual with appropriate expertise and experience in the specialist area or discipline relevant to the instruction or issue in dispute.

·8 ·2 Where the Adjudicator does not have the appropriate expertise and experience referred to in clause 41A·5·8·1 above the Adjudicator shall appoint an independent expert with such relevant expertise and experience to advise and report in writing on whether or not any instruction issued under clause 8·4·4 is reasonable in all the circumstances.

·8 ·3 Where an expert has been appointed by the Adjudicator pursuant to clause 41A·5·8·2 above the Parties shall be jointly and severally responsible for the expert's fees and expenses but, in his decision, the Adjudicator shall direct as to who should pay the fees and expenses of such expert or the proportion in which such fees and expenses are to be shared between the Parties.

·8 ·4 Notwithstanding the provisions of clause 41A·5·4 above, where an independent expert has been appointed by the Adjudicator pursuant to clause 41A·5·8·2 above, copies of the Adjudicator's instructions to the expert and any written advice or reports received from such expert shall be supplied to the Parties as soon as practicable.

Adjudicator's fee and reasonable expenses – payment

41A·6 ·1 The Adjudicator in his decision shall state how payment of his fee and reasonable expenses is to be apportioned as between the Parties. In default of such statement the Parties shall bear the cost of the Adjudicator's fee and reasonable expenses in equal proportions.

41A·6 ·2 The Parties shall be jointly and severally liable to the Adjudicator for his fee and for all expenses reasonably incurred by the Adjudicator pursuant to the adjudication.

Effect of Adjudicator's decision

41A·7 ·1 The decision of the Adjudicator shall be binding on the Parties until the dispute or difference is finally determined by arbitration or by legal proceedings [xx] or by an agreement in writing between the Parties made after the decision of the Adjudicator has been given.

41A·7 ·2 The Parties shall, without prejudice to their other rights under this Contract, comply with the decision of the Adjudicator; and the Employer and the Contractor shall ensure that the decision of the Adjudicator is given effect.

41A·7 ·3 If either Party does not comply with the decision of the Adjudicator the other Party shall be entitled to take legal proceedings to secure such compliance pending any final determination of the referred dispute or difference pursuant to clause 41A·7·1.

Immunity

41A·8 The Adjudicator shall not be liable for anything done or omitted in the discharge or purported discharge of his functions as Adjudicator unless the act or omission is in bad faith and this protection from liability shall similarly extend to any employee or agent of the Adjudicator.

41B Arbitration

A reference in clause 41B to a Rule or Rules is a reference to the JCT 1998 edition of the Construction Industry Model Arbitration Rules (CIMAR) current at the Base Date.

41B·1 ·1 Where pursuant to article 7A either Party requires a dispute or difference to be referred to arbitration then that Party shall serve on the other Party a notice of arbitration to such effect in accordance with Rule 2.1 which states:

"Arbitral proceedings are begun in respect of a dispute when one party serves on the other a written notice of arbitration identifying the dispute and requiring him to agree to the appointment of an arbitrator";

Footnote

[xx] The arbitration or legal proceedings are **not** an appeal against the decision of the Adjudicator but are a consideration of the dispute or difference as if no decision had been made by an Adjudicator.

41B·1 ·1 *continued*

and an arbitrator shall be an individual agreed by the Parties or appointed by the person named in the Appendix in accordance with Rule 2.3 which states:

> "If the parties fail to agree on the name of an arbitrator within 14 days (or any agreed extension) after:
> (i) the notice of arbitration is served, or
> (ii) a previously appointed arbitrator ceases to hold office for any reason,
> either party may apply for the appointment of an arbitrator to the person so empowered."

By Rule 2.5:

> "the arbitrator's appointment takes effect upon his agreement to act or his appointment under Rule 2.3, whether or not his terms have been accepted."

41B·1 ·2 Where two or more related arbitral proceedings in respect of the Works fall under separate arbitration agreements, Rules 2.6, 2.7 and 2.8 shall apply thereto.

41B·1 ·3 After an arbitrator has been appointed either Party may give a further notice of arbitration to the other Party and to the Arbitrator referring any other dispute which falls under article 7A to be decided in the arbitral proceedings and Rule 3.3 shall apply thereto.

41B·2 Subject to the provisions of article 7A and clause 30·9 the Arbitrator shall, without prejudice to the generality of his powers, have power to rectify this Contract so that it accurately reflects the true agreement made by the Parties, to direct such measurements and/or valuations as may in his opinion be desirable in order to determine the rights of the Parties and to ascertain and award any sum which ought to have been the subject of or included in any certificate and to open up, review and revise any certificate, opinion, decision, requirement or notice and to determine all matters in dispute which shall be submitted to him in the same manner as if no such certificate, opinion, decision, requirement or notice had been given.

41B·3 Subject to clause 41B·4 the award of such Arbitrator shall be final and binding on the Parties.

41B·4 The Parties hereby agree pursuant to S. 45(2)(a) and S. 69(2)(a) of the Arbitration Act 1996 that either Party may (upon notice to the other Party and to the Arbitrator):

41B·4 ·1 apply to the courts to determine any question of law arising in the course of the reference; and

41B·4 ·2 appeal to the courts on any question of law arising out of an award made in an arbitration under this Arbitration Agreement.

41B·5 The provisions of the Arbitration Act 1996 or any amendment thereof shall apply to any arbitration under this Contract wherever the same, or any part of it, shall be conducted. [yy]

41B·6 The arbitration shall be conducted in accordance with the JCT 1998 edition of the Construction Industry Model Arbitration Rules (CIMAR) current at the Base Date. Provided that if any amendments to the Rules so current have been issued by the JCT after the Base Date the Parties may, by a joint notice in writing to the Arbitrator, state that they wish the arbitration to be conducted in accordance with the Rules as so amended.

41C   Legal proceedings

41C·1 Where article 7B applies any dispute or difference shall be determined by legal proceedings pursuant to article 7B.

Footnote

[yy] It should be noted that the provisions of the Arbitration Act 1996 do not extend to Scotland. Where the site of the Works is situated in Scotland then the forms issued by the Scottish Building Contract Committee which contain Scots proper law adjudication and arbitration provisions are the appropriate documents. The SBCC issues guidance in this respect.

Part 5: Performance Specified Work [zz]

Meaning of Performance Specified Work

42·1 The term 'Performance Specified Work' means work:

42·1 ·1 identified in the Appendix, and

42·1 ·2 which is to be provided by the Contractor, and

42·1 ·3 for which certain requirements have been predetermined and are shown on the Contract Drawings, and

42·1 ·4 in respect of which the performance which the Employer requires from such work and which the Contractor, by this Contract and subject to the Conditions, is required to achieve has been stated in the Contract Bills and these Bills have included

    either   information relating thereto sufficient to have enabled the Contractor to price such Performance Specified Work

    or   a provisional sum in respect of the Performance Specified Work together with the information relating thereto as referred to in clause 42·7.

Contractor's Statement

42·2 Before carrying out any Performance Specified Work, the Contractor shall provide the Architect with a document or set of documents, referred to in these Conditions as the 'Contractor's Statement'. Before so providing the Contractor shall have referred the draft of such Statement to the Planning Supervisor and shall have made such amendments, if any, as may have been necessary to take account of the comments of the Planning Supervisor. Subject to the Conditions the Contractor shall carry out the Performance Specified Work in accordance with that Statement.

Contents of Contractor's Statement

42·3 The Contractor's Statement shall be sufficient in form and detail adequately to explain the Contractor's proposals for the execution of the Performance Specified Work. It shall include any information which is required to be included therein by the Contract Bills or, where there is a provisional sum for the Performance Specified Work, by the instruction of the Architect on the expenditure of that sum; and may include information in drawn or scheduled form and a statement of calculations; and, if applicable, shall be provided in reasonable time so that the Architect can provide the information, drawings and details as he is required to provide pursuant to clauses 5·4·1 and 5·4·2.

Time for Contractor's Statement

42·4 The Contractor's Statement shall be provided to the Architect:

– by any date for its provision given in the Contract Bills or

– by any reasonable date for its provision given in the instruction by the Architect on the expenditure of a provisional sum for Performance Specified Work.

If no such date is given it shall be provided at a reasonable time before the Contractor intends to carry out the Performance Specified Work.

Architect's notice to amend Contractor's Statement

42·5 Within 14 days after receipt of the Contractor's Statement the Architect may, if he is of the opinion that such Statement is deficient in form and/or detail adequately to explain the Contractor's proposals for the execution of the Performance Specified Work, by notice in writing require the Contractor to amend such Statement so that it is in the opinion of the Architect not deficient. A copy of the Statement as so amended shall be provided to the Architect. Whether or not an amendment is required by the Architect, the Contractor is responsible in accordance with the Conditions for any deficiency in such Statement and for the Performance Specified Work to which such Statement refers.

Architect's notice of deficiency in Contractor's Statement

42·6 If the Architect shall find anything in the Contractor's Statement which appears to the Architect to be a deficiency which would adversely affect the performance required by the Employer from the relevant Performance Specified Work, he shall immediately give notice to the Contractor specifying the deficiency. Whether or not a notice is given by the Architect, the Contractor is responsible in accordance with the Conditions for the Performance Specified Work.

Footnote

[zz] See Practice Note 25 'Performance Specified Work' paragraphs 2·6 to 2·8 for a description of work which is not to be treated as Performance Specified Work.

Definition of provisional sum for Performance Specified Work	**42·7**	A provisional sum for Performance Specified Work means a sum provided in the Contract Bills for Performance Specified Work where the following information has been provided in the Contract Bills:
	42·7 ·1	the performance which the Employer requires from such work;
	42·7 ·2	the location of such Performance Specified Work in the building;
	42·7 ·3	information relating thereto sufficient to have enabled the Contractor to have made due allowance in programming for the execution of such Performance Specified Work and for pricing all preliminary items relevant to such Performance Specified Work.
Instructions of the Architect on other provisional sums	**42·8**	No instruction of the Architect pursuant to clause 13·3·1 on the expenditure of provisional sums included in the Contract Bills shall require Performance Specified Work except an instruction on the expenditure of a provisional sum included in the Contract Bills for Performance Specified Work.
Preparation of Contract Bills	**42·9**	The inclusion of Performance Specified Work in the Contract Bills shall not be regarded as a departure from the method of preparation of these Bills referred to in clause 2·2·2·1.
Provisional sum for Performance Specified Work – errors or omissions in Contract Bills	**42·10**	If in the Contract Bills there is any error or omission in the information which, pursuant to clause 42·7·2 and/or 42·7·3, is to be included in the Contract Bills in respect of a provisional sum for Performance Specified Work such error or omission shall be corrected so that it does provide such information; and any such correction shall be treated as if it were a Variation required by an instruction of the Architect under clause 13·2.
Variations in respect of Performance Specified Work	**42·11**	Subject to clause 42·12 the Architect may issue instructions under clause 13·2 requiring a Variation to Performance Specified Work.
Agreement for additional Performance Specified Work	**42·12**	No instruction of the Architect under clause 13·2 may require as a Variation the provision by the Contractor of Performance Specified Work additional to that which has been identified in the Appendix unless the Employer and the Contractor otherwise agree.
Analysis	**42·13**	Where the Contract Bills do not provide an analysis of the portion of the Contract Sum which relates to any Performance Specified Work the Contractor shall provide such an analysis ('the Analysis') within 14 days of being required to do so by the Architect.
Integration of Performance Specified Work	**42·14**	The Architect shall, within a reasonable time before the Contractor intends to carry out the Performance Specified Work, give any instructions necessary for the integration of such Performance Specified Work with the design of the Works. The Contractor shall, subject to clause 42·15, comply with any such instruction.
Compliance with Architect's instructions – Contractor's notice of injurious affection	**42·15**	If the Contractor is of the opinion that compliance with any instruction of the Architect injuriously affects the efficacy of the Performance Specified Work, he shall within 7 days of receipt of the relevant instruction specify by notice in writing to the Architect such injurious affection. Except where the Architect amends the instruction to remove such injurious affection, the instruction shall not have effect without the written consent of the Contractor which consent shall not be unreasonably delayed or withheld.
Delay by Contractor in providing the Contractor's Statement	**42·16**	Except for any extension of time in respect of the Relevant Event stated in clause 25·4·15 an extension of time shall not be given under clause 25·3 and clauses 26·1 and 28·2·2 shall not have effect where and to the extent that the cause of the progress of the Works having been delayed, affected or suspended is that the Architect has not received the Contractor's Statement by the time referred to in clause 42·4 or any amendment to the Contractor's Statement pursuant to clause 42·5.
Performance Specified Work – Contractor's obligation	**42·17 ·1**	The Contractor shall exercise reasonable skill and care in the provision of Performance Specified Work provided that:
	·1 ·1	clause 42·17 shall not be construed so as to affect the obligations of the Contractor under this Contract in regard to the supply of workmanship, materials and goods; and
	·1 ·2	nothing in this Contract shall operate as a guarantee of fitness for purpose of the Performance Specified Work.
	42·17 ·2	The Contractor's obligation under clause 42·17·1 shall in no way be modified by any service in respect of any Performance Specified Work which he has obtained from others and, in particular, the Contractor shall be responsible for any such service as if such services had been undertaken by the Contractor himself.

Nomination excluded

42·18 Performance Specified Work pursuant to clause 42 shall not be provided by a Nominated Sub-Contractor under a Nominated Sub-Contract or by a Nominated Supplier under a contract of sale to which clause 36 refers.

Code of Practice: referred to in clause 8·4·4

1 This is the Code of Practice referred to in clause 8·4·4. The purpose of the Code is to help in the fair and reasonable operation of the requirements of clause 8·4·4.

2 The Architect and the Contractor should endeavour to agree the amount and method of opening up or testing but in any case in issuing his instructions pursuant to clause 8·4·4 the Architect is required to consider the following criteria:

·1 the need in the event of non-compliance to demonstrate at no cost to the Employer either that it is unique and not likely to occur in similar elements of the Works or alternatively the extent of any similar non-compliance in the Works already constructed or still to be constructed;

·2 the need to discover whether any non-compliance in a primary structural element is a failure of workmanship and/or materials such that rigorous testing of similar elements must take place; or where the non-compliance is in a less significant element whether it is such as is to be statistically expected and can be simply repaired; or whether the non-compliance indicates an inherent weakness such as can only be found by selective testing the extent of which must depend upon the importance of any detail concerned;

·3 the significance of the non-compliance having regard to the nature of the work in which it has occurred;

·4 the consequence of any similar non-compliance on the safety of the building, its effect on users, adjoining property, the public, and compliance with any Statutory Requirements;

·5 the level and standard of supervision and control of the Works by the Contractor;

·6 the relevant records of the Contractor and where relevant of any sub-contractor resulting from the supervision and control referred to in paragraph 2·5 above or otherwise;

·7 any Codes of Practice or similar advice issued by a responsible body which are applicable to the non-complying work, materials or goods;

·8 any failure by the Contractor to carry out, or to secure the carrying out of, any tests specified in the Contract Documents or in an instruction of the Architect;

·9 the reason for the non-compliance when this has been established;

·10 any technical advice that the Contractor has obtained in respect of the non-complying work, materials or goods;

·11 current recognised testing procedures;

·12 the practicability of progressive testing in establishing whether any similar non-compliance is reasonably likely;

·13 if alternative testing methods are available, the time required for and the consequential costs of such alternative testing methods;

·14 any proposals of the Contractor;

·15 any other relevant matters.

Appendix

Clause etc.	Subject	
Fourth recital and 31	Construction Industry Scheme (CIS)	Employer at the Base Date *is a 'contractor'/is not a 'contractor' for the purposes of the Act and the Regulations
Fifth recital	CDM Regulations	*All the CDM Regulations apply/ Regulations 7 and 13 only of the CDM Regulations apply
Articles 7A and 7B 41B 41C	Dispute or difference – settlement of disputes	*Clause 41B applies *Delete if disputes are to be decided by legal proceedings and article 7B is thus to apply
1·3	Base Date	_____
1·3	Date for Completion	_____
1·11	Electronic data interchange	The JCT Supplemental Provisions for EDI *apply/do not apply If applicable: the EDI Agreement to which the Supplemental Provisions refer is: *the EDI Association Standard EDI Agreement *the European Model EDI Agreement
15·2	VAT Agreement	Clause 1A of the VAT Agreement *applies/does not apply [x]
17·2	Defects Liability Period (if none other stated is 6 months from the day named in the certificate of Practical Completion of the Works)	_____
19·1·2	Assignment by Employer of benefits after Practical Completion	Clause 19·1·2 *applies/does not apply
21·1·1	Insurance cover for any one occurrence or series of occurrences arising out of one event	£ _____
21·2·1	Insurance – liability of Employer	Insurance *may be required/is not required Amount of indemnity for any one occurrence or series of occurrences arising out of one event £ _____ [aaa]

Footnotes

*Delete as applicable.

[x] Clause 1A can only apply where the Contractor is satisfied at the date the Contract is entered into that his output tax on **all** supplies to the Employer under the Contract will be at either a positive or a zero rate of tax.

This footnote repeats footnote [x] for clause 15·2.

[aaa] If the indemnity is to be for an aggregate amount and not for any one occurrence or series of occurrences the entry should make this clear.

Clause etc.	Subject	
22·1	Insurance of the Works – alternative clauses	*Clause 22A/Clause 22B/Clause 22C applies (See footnote [cc] to clause 22)
*22A, 22B·1, 22C·2	Percentage to cover professional fees	_____
22A·3·1	Annual renewal date of insurance as supplied by Contractor	_____
22D	Insurance for Employer's loss of liquidated damages – clause 25·4·3	Insurance *may be required/is not required
22D·2		Period of time _____
22FC·1	Joint Fire Code	The Joint Fire Code *applies/does not apply If the Joint Fire Code is applicable, state whether the insurer under clause 22A or clause 22B or clause 22C·2 has specified that the Works are a 'Large Project': *YES/NO (where clause 22A applies these entries are made on information supplied by the Contractor)
22FC·5	Joint Fire Code – amendments/revisions	The cost, if any, of compliance with amendment(s) or revision(s) to the Joint Fire Code shall be borne by *the Employer/the Contractor
23·1·1	Date of Possession	_____
23·1·2, 25·4·13, 26·1	Deferment of the Date of Possession	Clause 23·1·2 *applies/does not apply Period of deferment if it is to be less than 6 weeks is _____
24·2	Liquidated and ascertained damages	at the rate of £ _____ per _____
28·2·2	Period of suspension (if none stated is 1 month)	_____
28A·1·1·1 to 28A·1·1·3	Period of suspension (if none stated is 3 months)	_____
28A·1·1·4 to 28A·1·1·6	Period of suspension (if none stated is 1 month)	_____

Footnote   *Delete as applicable.

Clause etc.	Subject	
30·1·1·6	Advance payment	Clause 30·1·1·6 *applies/does not apply If applicable: the advance payment will be **£ _____ / _____ % of the Contract Sum and will be paid to the Contractor on _____ and will be reimbursed to the Employer in the following amount(s) and at the following time(s) _____ _____ _____ _____ An advance payment bond *is/is not required
30·1·3	Dates of issue of Interim Certificates (if none stated, Interim Certificates are to be issued at intervals not exceeding one month up to the date of Practical Completion or within one month thereafter and the first Interim Certificate is to be issued within one month of the Date of Possession)	The first date is: _____ and thereafter on the same date in each month adjusted to the nearest working day in that month [aaa·1]
30·2·1·1	Gross valuation	A priced Activity Schedule *is/is not attached to this Appendix
30·3·1	Listed items – uniquely identified	*For uniquely identified listed items a bond as referred to in clause 30·3·1 in respect of payment for such items is required for £ _____ *Delete if no bond is required
30·3·2	Listed items – not uniquely identified	*For listed items that are not uniquely identified a bond as referred to in clause 30·3·2 in respect of payment for such items is required for £ _____ *Delete if clause 30·3·2 does not apply

Footnotes

*Delete as applicable.

**Insert either a money amount or a percentage figure and delete the other alternative.

[aaa·1] The first date should not be more than one month after the Date of Possession. Where it is intended that Interim Certificates be issued on the last day of each month consider inserting "the last day of _____ *(insert month)* and thereafter the last day in each month adjusted to the nearest working day in the month".

Clause etc.	Subject	
30·4·1·1	Retention Percentage (if less than 5 per cent) [bbb]	
30·4A	Contractor's bond in lieu of Retention	Clause 30·4A *applies/does not apply
30·4A·2		If clause 30·4A applies: clause 2 of the bond maximum aggregate sum is: £ _____ clause 6(iii) of the bond the expiry date is _____
35·2	Work reserved for Nominated Sub-Contractors for which the Contractor desires to tender	_____
37	Fluctuations: (if alternative required is not shown clause 38 shall apply)	clause 38 [ccc] clause 39 clause 40
38·7 or 39·8	Percentage addition	_____
40·1·1·1	Formula Rules	rule 3: Base Month _____ 20 _____ rules 10 and 30(i): Part I/Part II [ddd] of Section 2 of the Formula Rules is to apply
41A·2	Adjudication – nominator of Adjudicator (if no nominator is selected the nominator shall be the President or a Vice-President of the Royal Institute of British Architects; if the nominator fails to nominate, the nominator shall be one of the other listed nominators selected by the Party requiring the reference to adjudication)	President or a Vice-President or Chairman or a Vice-Chairman: *Royal Institute of British Architects *Royal Institution of Chartered Surveyors *Construction Confederation *National Specialist Contractors Council *Delete all but one
41B·1	Arbitration – appointor of Arbitrator (if no appointor is selected the appointor shall be the President or a Vice-President of the Royal Institute of British Architects)	President or a Vice-President: *Royal Institute of British Architects *Royal Institution of Chartered Surveyors *Chartered Institute of Arbitrators *Delete all but one
42·1·1	Performance Specified Work	Identify below or on a separate sheet each item of Performance Specified Work to be provided by the Contractor and insert the relevant reference in the Contract Bills [zz]

Footnotes

[bbb] The percentage will be 5 per cent unless a lower rate is specified here.

[ccc] Delete alternatives not used.

[ddd] Strike out according to which method of formula adjustment (Part I – Work Category Method or Part II – Work Group Method) has been stated in the documents issued to tenderers.

[zz] See Practice Note 25 'Performance Specified Work' paragraphs 2·6 to 2·8 for a description of work which is **not** to be treated as Performance Specified Work.

This footnote repeats footnote [zz] *for clause 42.*

Annex 1 to Appendix: Terms of Bonds
agreed by the JCT and the British Bankers' Association

See clause 30·1·1·6:
"Advance Payment Bond", and

clause 30·3:
"Bond in respect of payment for off-site materials and/or goods"

Advance Payment Bond

1 THE parties to this Bond are:

(1) _____

whose registered office is at _____

_____ ('the Surety'), and

(2) _____

of _____

_____ ('the Employer').

2 The Employer and _____ ('the Contractor')

have agreed to enter into a contract for building works ('the Works') at _____

_____ ('the Contract').

3 The Employer has agreed to pay the Contractor the sum of [_____] as an advance payment of sums due to the Contractor under the Contract ('the Advance Payment') for reimbursement by the Surety on the following terms:

(a) When the Surety receives a demand from the Employer in accordance with clause 3(b) the Surety shall repay the Employer the sum demanded up to the amount of the Advance Payment.

(b) The Employer shall in making any demand provide to the Surety a completed notice of demand in the form of the **Schedule** attached hereto which shall be accepted as conclusive evidence for all purposes under this Bond. The signatures on any such demand must be authenticated by the Employer's bankers.

(c) The Surety shall within 5 Business Days after receiving the demand pay to the Employer the sum so demanded. 'Business Day' means the day (other than a Saturday or a Sunday) on which commercial banks are open for business in London.

4 Payments due under this Bond shall be made notwithstanding any dispute between the Employer and the Contractor and whether or not the Employer and the Contractor are or might be under any liability one to the other. Payment by the Surety under this Bond shall be deemed a valid payment for all purposes of this Bond and shall discharge the Surety from liability to the extent of such payment.

5 The Surety consents and agrees that the following actions by the Employer may be made and done without notice to or consent of the Surety and without in any way affecting changing or releasing the Surety from its obligations under this Bond and the liability of the Surety hereunder shall not in any way be affected hereby. The actions are:

(a) waiver by the Employer of any of the terms, provisions, conditions, obligations and agreements of the Contractor or any failure to make demand upon or take action against the Contractor;

(b) any modification or changes to the Contract; and/or

(c) the granting of any extensions of time to the Contractor without affecting the terms of clause 7(c) below.

6 The Surety's maximum aggregate liability under this Bond which shall commence on payment of the Advance Payment by the Employer to the Contractor shall be the amount of [_____] which sum shall be reduced by the amount of any reimbursement made by the Contractor to the Employer as advised by the Employer in writing to the Surety.

7 The obligations of the Surety and under this Bond shall cease upon whichever is the earliest of:

(a) the date on which the Advance Payment is reduced to nil as certified in writing to the Surety by the Employer;

(b) the date on which the Advance Payment or any balance thereof is repaid to the Employer by the Contractor (as certified in writing to the Surety by the Employer) or by the Surety; and

(c) [*longstop date to be given*],

and any claims hereunder must be received by the Surety in writing on or before such earliest date.

8 This Bond is not transferable or assignable without the prior written consent of the Surety. Such written consent will not be unreasonably withheld.

9 Notwithstanding any other provisions of this Bond nothing in this Bond confers or purports to confer any right to enforce any of its terms on any person who is not a party to it.

10 This Bond shall be governed and construed in accordance with the laws of England and Wales.

IN WITNESS hereof this Bond has been executed as a Deed by the Surety and delivered on the date below:

EXECUTED as a Deed by: _____

for and on behalf of the Surety: _____

EXECUTED as a Deed by: _____

for and on behalf of the Employer: _____

Date: _____

Schedule to Advance Payment Bond
(clause 3(b) of the Bond)

Notice of Demand

Date of Notice: _____

Date of Bond: _____

Employer: _____

Surety: _____

The Bond has come into effect.

We hereby demand payment of the sum of

£ _____ (amount in words)
which does not exceed the amount of reimbursement for which the Contractor is in default at the date of this notice.

Address for payment: _____

_____

This Notice is signed by the following persons who are authorised by the Employer to act for and on his behalf:

Signed by _____

    Name: _____

    Official Position: _____

Signed by _____

    Name: _____

    Official Position: _____

The above signatures to be authenticated by the Employer's bankers

Bond in respect of payment for off-site materials and/or goods

1. THE parties to this Bond are:

   (1) _____

   whose registered office is at _____

   _____ ('the Surety'), and

   (2) _____

   of _____

   _____ ('the Employer').

2. The Employer and _____ ('the Contractor')

   have agreed to enter into a building contract for building works ('the Works')

   at _____ ('the Contract').

3. Subject to the relevant provisions of the Contract as summarised below but with which the Surety shall not at all be concerned:

   (a) the Employer has agreed to include in the amount stated as due in Interim Certificates (as defined in the Contract) for payment by the Employer the value of those materials or goods or items pre-fabricated for inclusion in the Works which have been listed by the Employer which list ('the listed items'), has been included as part of the Contract, before their delivery to or adjacent to the Works; and

   (b) the Contractor has agreed to insure the listed items against loss or damage for their full value under a policy of insurance protecting the interests of the Employer and the Contractor during the period commencing with the transfer of the property in the items to the Contractor until they are delivered to or adjacent to the Works; and

   (c) this Bond shall exclusively relate to the amount paid to the Contractor in respect of the listed items which have not been delivered to or adjacent to the Works.

4. The Employer shall in making any demand provide to the Surety a Notice of Demand in the form of the **Schedule** attached hereto which shall be accepted as conclusive evidence for all purposes under this Bond. The signatures on any such demand must be authenticated by the Employer's bankers.

5. The Surety shall within 5 Business Days after receiving the demand pay to the Employer the sum so demanded. 'Business Day' means the day (other than a Saturday or a Sunday) on which commercial banks are open for business in London.

6. Payments due under this Bond shall be made notwithstanding any dispute between the Employer and the Contractor and whether or not the Employer and the Contractor are or might be under any liability one to the other. Payment by the Surety under this Bond shall be deemed a valid payment for all purposes of this Bond and shall discharge the Surety from liability to the extent of such payment.

7   The Surety consents and agrees that the following actions by the Employer may be made and done without notice to or consent of the Surety and without in any way affecting changing or releasing the Surety from its obligations under this Bond and the liability of the Surety hereunder shall not in any way be affected hereby. The actions are:

   (a) waiver by the Employer of any of the terms, provisions, conditions, obligations and agreements of the Contractor or any failure to make demand upon or take action against the Contractor;

   (b) any modification or changes to the Contract; and/or

   (c) the granting of an extension of time to the Contractor without affecting the terms of clause 9(b) below.

8   The Surety's maximum aggregate liability under this Bond shall be * [_____].

9   The obligations of the Surety under this Bond shall cease upon whichever is the earlier of

   (a) the date on which all the listed items have been delivered to or adjacent to the Works as certified in writing to the Surety by the Employer; and

   (b) [longstop date to be given],

   and any claims hereunder must be received by the Surety in writing on or before such earlier date.

10 The Bond is not transferable or assignable without the prior written consent of the Surety. Such written consent will not be unreasonably withheld.

11 Notwithstanding any other provisions of this Bond nothing in this Bond confers or purports to confer any right to enforce any of its terms on any person who is not a party to it.

12 This Bond shall be governed and construed in accordance with the laws of England and Wales.

*The value stated in the Contract which the Employer considers will be sufficient to cover him for maximum payments to the Contractor for the listed items that will have been made and not delivered to the site at any one time.

IN WITNESS hereof this Bond has been executed as a Deed by the Surety and delivered on the date below:

EXECUTED as a Deed by: _____

   for and on behalf of the Surety: _____

EXECUTED as a Deed by: _____

   for and on behalf of the Employer: _____

Date: _____

Schedule to Bond
(clause 4 of the Bond)

Notice of Demand

Date of Notice: _____

Date of Bond: _____

Employer: _____

Surety: _____

We hereby demand payment of the sum of £_____
being the amount stated as due in respect of listed items included in the amount stated as due in an Interim Certificate(s) for payment which has been duly made to the Contractor by the Employer but such listed items have not been delivered to or adjacent to the Works.

Address for payment: _____

_____

This Notice is signed by the following persons who are authorised by the Employer to act for and on his behalf:

Signed by _____

    Name: _____

    Official Position: _____

Signed by _____

    Name: _____

    Official Position: _____

The above signatures to be authenticated by the Employer's bankers

Supplemental Provisions
(the VAT Agreement)

The following are the supplemental provisions (the VAT Agreement) referred to in clause 15·1 of the Conditions:

Interim payments – addition of VAT

1 The Employer shall pay to the Contractor in the manner hereinafter set out any tax properly chargeable by the Commissioners on the Contractor on the supply to the Employer of any goods and services by the Contractor under this Contract. Supplies of goods and services under this Contract are supplies under a contract providing for periodical payment for such supplies within the meaning of Regulation 93 of the Value Added Tax Regulations 1995 or any amendment or re-enactment thereof.

Alternative provisions to clauses 1·1 to 1·2·2 inclusive

1A·1 Where it is stated in the Appendix pursuant to clause 15·2 of the Conditions that clause 1A of this Agreement applies clauses 1·1 to 1·2·2 inclusive hereof shall not apply unless and until any notice issued under clause 1A·4 hereof becomes effective or unless the Contractor fails to give the written notice required under clause 1A·2. Where clause 1A applies clauses 1 and 1·3 to 8 of this Agreement remain in full force and effect.

1A·2 Not later than 7 days before the date for the issue of the first Interim Certificate the Contractor shall give written notice to the Employer, with a copy to the Architect, of the rate of tax chargeable on the supply of goods and services for which Interim Certificates and the Final Certificate are to be issued. If the rate of tax so notified is varied under statute the Contractor shall, not later than 7 days after the date when such varied rate comes into effect, send to the Employer, with a copy to the Architect, the necessary amendment to the rate given in his written notice and that notice shall then take effect as so amended.

1A·3 For the purpose of complying with the VAT Agreement for the recovery by the Contractor, as stated in clause 15·2 of the Conditions, from the Employer of tax properly chargeable by the Commissioners on the Contractor, an amount calculated at the rate given in the aforesaid written notice (or, where relevant, amended written notice) shall be shown on each Interim Certificate issued by the Architect and, unless the procedure set out in clause 1·3 hereof shall have been completed, on the Final Certificate issued by the Architect. Such amount shall be paid by the Employer to the Contractor or by the Contractor to the Employer as the case may be within the period for payment of certificates set out in clause 30·1·1·1 *(Interim Certificates)* or clause 30·8 *(Final Certificate)* as applicable.

1A·4 Either the Employer or the Contractor may give written notice to the other, with a copy to the Architect, stating that with effect from the date of the notice clause 1A shall no longer apply. From that date the provisions of clauses 1·1 to 1·2·2 inclusive hereof shall apply in place of clause 1A hereof.

Written assessment by Contractor

1·1 Unless clause 1A applies the Contractor shall not later than the date for the issue of each Interim Certificate and, unless the procedure set out in clause 1·3 of this Agreement shall have been completed, for the issue of the Final Certificate give to the Employer a written provisional assessment of the respective values (less any Retention Percentage applicable thereto) of those supplies of goods and services for which the Certificate is being issued and which will be chargeable, at the relevant time of supply under Regulation 93 of the Value Added Tax Regulations 1995 on the Contractor at

1·1 ·1 a zero rate of tax (Category (i)) and

1·1 ·2 any rate or rates of tax other than zero (Category (ii)).

The Contractor shall also specify the rate or rates of tax which are chargeable on those supplies included in Category (ii), and shall state the grounds on which he considers such supplies are so chargeable.

Employer to calculate amount of tax due – Employer's right of reasonable objection

1·2 ·1 Upon receipt of such written provisional assessment the Employer, unless he has reasonable grounds for objection to that assessment, shall calculate the amount of tax due by applying the rate or rates of tax specified by the Contractor to the amount of the assessed value of those supplies included in Category (ii) of such assessment, and remit the calculated amount of such tax, together with the amount of the Certificate issued by the Architect, to the Contractor within the period for payment of certificates set out in clause 30·1·1·1 of the Conditions.

1·2 ·2 If the Employer has reasonable grounds for objection to the provisional assessment he shall within 3 working days of receipt of that assessment so notify the Contractor in writing setting out those grounds. The Contractor shall within 3 working days of receipt of the written notification of the Employer reply in writing to the Employer either that he withdraws the assessment in which case the Employer is released from his obligation under clause 1·2·1 of this Agreement or that he confirms the assessment. If the Contractor so confirms then the Contractor may treat any amount received from the Employer in respect of the value which the Contractor has stated to be chargeable on him at a rate or rates of tax other than zero as being inclusive of tax and issue an authenticated receipt under clause 1·4 of this Agreement.

Written final statement – VAT liability of Contractor – recovery from Employer

1·3 ·1 Where clause 1A is operated clause 1·3 only applies if no amount of tax pursuant to clause 1A·3 has been shown on the Final Certificate issued by the Architect. After the issue of the Certificate of Completion of Making Good Defects under clause 17·4 of the Conditions the Contractor shall as soon as he can finally so ascertain prepare a written final statement of the respective values of all supplies of goods and services for which certificates have been or will be issued which are chargeable on the Contractor at

    ·1 ·1 a zero rate of tax (Category (i)) and

    ·1 ·2 any rate or rates of tax other than zero (Category (ii))

and shall issue such final statement to the Employer.

The Contractor shall also specify the rate or rates of tax which are chargeable on the value of those supplies included in Category (ii) and shall state the grounds on which he considers such supplies are so chargeable.

The Contractor shall also state the total amount of tax already received by the Contractor for which a receipt or receipts under clause 1·4 of this Agreement have been issued.

1·3 ·2 The statement under clause 1·3·1 of this Agreement may be issued either before or after the issue of the Final Certificate under clause 30·8 of the Conditions.

1·3 ·3 Upon receipt of the written final statement the Employer shall, subject to clause 3 of this Agreement, calculate the final amount of tax due by applying the rate or rates of tax specified by the Contractor to the value of those supplies included in Category (ii) of the statement and deducting therefrom the total amount of tax already received by the Contractor specified in the statement, and shall pay the balance of such tax to the Contractor within 28 days from receipt of the statement.

1·3 ·4 If the Employer finds that the total amount of tax specified in the final statement as already paid by him exceeds the amount of tax calculated under clause 1·3·3 of this Agreement the Employer shall so notify the Contractor who shall refund such excess to the Employer within 28 days of receipt of the notification, together with a receipt under clause 1·4 of this Agreement showing the correction of the amounts for which a receipt or receipts have previously been issued by the Contractor.

Contractor to issue receipt as tax invoice

1·4 Upon receipt of any amount paid under certificates of the Architect and any tax properly paid under the provisions of clause 1 or clause 1A of this Agreement the Contractor shall issue to the Employer a receipt of the kind referred to in Regulation 13(4) of the Value Added Tax Regulations 1995 containing the particulars required under Regulation 14 of the aforesaid Regulations or any amendment or re-enactment thereof to be contained in a tax invoice.

Value of supply – liquidated damages to be disregarded

2·1 If, when the Employer is obliged to make payment under clause 1·2 or 1·3 of this Agreement, he is empowered under clause 24 of the Conditions to deduct any sum calculated at the rate stated in the Appendix as liquidated and ascertained damages from sums due or to become due to the Contractor under this Contract he shall disregard any such deduction in calculating the tax due on the value of goods and services supplied to which he is obliged to add tax under clause 1·2 or 1·3 of this Agreement.

2·2 The Contractor when ascertaining the respective values of any supplies of goods and services for which certificates have been or will be issued under the Conditions in order to prepare the final statement referred to in clause 1·3 of this Agreement shall disregard when stating such values any deduction by the Employer of any sum calculated at the rate stated in the Appendix as liquidated and ascertained damages under clause 24 of the Conditions.

2·3 Where clause 1A is operated the Employer shall pay the tax to which that clause refers notwithstanding any deduction which the Employer may be empowered to make under clause 24 of the Conditions from the amount certified by the Architect in an Interim Certificate or from any balance certified by the Architect as due to the Contractor under the Final Certificate.

Employers' right to challenge tax claimed by Contractor

3·1 If the Employer disagrees with the final statement issued by the Contractor under clause 1·3 of this Agreement he may but before any payment or refund becomes due under clause 1·3·3 or 1·3·4 of this Agreement request the Contractor to obtain the decision of the Commissioners on the tax properly chargeable on the Contractor for all supplies of goods and services under this Contract and the Contractor shall forthwith request the Commissioners for such decision. If the Employer disagrees with such decision then, provided the Employer indemnifies and at the option of the Contractor secures the Contractor against all costs and other expenses, the Contractor shall in accordance with the instructions of the Employer make all such appeals against the decision of the commissioners as the Employer shall request. The Contractor shall account for any costs awarded in his favour in any appeals to which clause 3 of this Agreement applies.

3·2 Where, before any appeal from the decision of the Commissioners can proceed, the full amount of the tax alleged to be chargeable on the Contractor on the supply of goods and services under the Conditions must be paid or accounted for by the Contractor, the Employer shall pay to the Contractor the full amount of tax needed to comply with any such obligation.

3·3 Within 28 days of the final adjudication of an appeal (or of the date of the decision of the Commissioners if the Employer does not request the Contractor to refer such decision to appeal) the Employer or the Contractor, as the case may be, shall pay or refund to the other in accordance with such final adjudication any tax underpaid or overpaid, as the case may be, under the provisions of this Agreement and the provisions of clause 1·3·4 of this Agreement shall apply in regard to the provision of authenticated receipts.

Discharge of Employer from liability to pay tax to the Contractor

4 Upon receipt by the Contractor from the Employer or by the Employer from the Contractor, as the case may be, of any payment under clause 1·3·3 or 1·3·4 of this Agreement or where clause 1A of this Agreement is operated of any payment of the amount of tax shown upon the Final Certificate issued by the Architect, or upon final adjudication of any appeal made in accordance with the provisions of clause 3 of this Agreement and any resultant payment or refund under clause 3·3 of this Agreement, the Employer shall be discharged from any further liability to pay tax to the Contractor in accordance with the VAT Agreement. Provided always that if after the date of discharge under clause 4 of this Agreement the Commissioners decide to correct the tax due from the Contract on the supply to the Employer of any goods and services by the Contractor under this Contract the amount of any such correction shall be an additional payment by the Employer to the Contractor or by the Contractor to the Employer, as the case may be. The provisions of clause 3 of this Agreement in regard to disagreement with any decision of the Commissioners shall apply to any decision referred to in this proviso.

Awards in dispute procedures

5 If any dispute or difference is referred to adjudication or to arbitration pursuant to article 7A or to legal proceedings, then, insofar as any payment awarded in such adjudication or arbitration or legal proceedings varies the amount certified for payment for goods or services supplied by the Contractor to the Employer under this Contract or is an amount which ought to have been so certified but was not so certified, the provisions of this Agreement shall so far as relevant and applicable apply to any such payments.

Arbitration provision excluded

6 The provisions of article 7A shall not apply to any matters to be dealt with under clause 3 of this Agreement.

Employer's right where receipt not provided

7 Notwithstanding any provisions to the contrary elsewhere in the Conditions the Employer shall not be obliged to make any further payment to the Contractor under the Conditions if the Contractor is in default in providing the receipt referred to in clause 1·4 of this Agreement. Provided that clause 7 of this Agreement shall only apply where:

7 ·1 the Employer can show that he requires such receipt to validate any claim for credit for tax paid or payable under this Agreement which the Employer is entitled to make to the Commissioners, and

7 **·2** the Employer has

>paid tax in accordance with the provisional assessment of the Contractor under clause 1 of this Agreement unless he has sustained a reasonable objection under clause 1·2 of this Agreement; or

>paid tax in accordance with clause 1A of this Agreement.

VAT on determination

8 Where clause 27·4 of the Conditions becomes operative there shall be added to the amount allowable or payable to the Employer in addition to the amounts certified by the Architect any additional tax that the Employer has had to pay by reason of determination under clause 27 of the Conditions as compared with the tax the Employer would have paid if the determination had not occurred.

Annex 2 to the Conditions: Supplemental Provisions for EDI

(clause 1·11)

The following are the Supplemental Provisions for EDI referred to in clause 1·11 of the Conditions.

1 The Parties no later than when there is a binding contract between the Employer and the Contractor shall have entered into the Electronic Data Interchange Agreement identified in the Appendix ('the EDI Agreement'), which shall apply to the exchange of communications under this Contract subject to the following:

·1 except where expressly provided for in these provisions, nothing contained in the EDI Agreement shall override or modify the application or interpretation of this Contract;

·2 the types and classes of communication to which the EDI Agreement shall apply ('the Data') and the persons between whom the Data shall be exchanged are as stated in the Contract Documents or as subsequently agreed in writing between the Parties;

·3 the Adopted Protocol/EDI Message Standards and the User Manual/Technical Annex* are as stated in the Contract Documents or as subsequently agreed in writing between the Parties;

·4 where the Contract Documents require a type or class of communication to which the EDI Agreement applies to be in writing it shall be validly made if exchanged in accordance with the EDI Agreement except that the following shall not be valid unless in writing in accordance with the relevant provisions of this Contract:

·4 ·1 any determination of the employment of the Contractor;

·4 ·2 any suspension by the Contractor of the performance of his obligations under this Contract to the Employer;

·4 ·3 the Final Certificate;

·4 ·4 any invoking by either Party of the procedures applicable under this Contract to the resolution of disputes or differences;

·4 ·5 any agreement between the Parties amending the Conditions or these provisions.

2 The procedures applicable under this Contract to the resolution of disputes or differences shall apply to any dispute or difference concerning these provisions or the exchange of any Data under the EDI Agreement and any dispute resolution provisions in the EDI Agreement shall not apply to such disputes or differences.

Footnote * The EDI Association Standard EDI Agreement refers to an Adopted Protocol and User Manual; the European Model EDI Agreement refers to EDI Message Standards and a Technical Annex. Delete whichever is not applicable.

Annex 3 to the Conditions: Bond in lieu of Retention

See Note 1

BOND dated the _____ day of _____ 20 _____

issued by _____

of _____

_____ (hereinafter called 'the Surety')

in favour of _____

of _____

_____ (hereinafter called 'the Employer')

1 By a building contract ('the Contract') between the Employer and

_____

of _____

_____ (hereinafter called the 'Contractor')

the Employer has agreed that he will not exercise his right under the Contract to deduct Retention from amounts included in Interim Certificates provided the Contractor has taken out this Bond in favour of the Employer.

See Note 2

2 The Surety is hereby bound to the Employer in the maximum aggregate sum of

_____ (figures and words)

until the Surety is notified by the Employer in writing of the date of issue of the next Interim Certificate after Practical Completion when the maximum aggregate sum shall be reduced by 50 per cent.

3 The Employer shall, on a demand which complies with the requirements in clause 4, be entitled to receive from the Surety the sum therein demanded.

4   Any demand by the Employer under clause 3 shall:

   (i)   be in writing addressed to the Surety at its office at

   _____

   refer to this Bond, and with the signature(s) therein authenticated by the Employer's bankers; and

   (ii) state the amount of the Retention that would have been held by the Employer at the date of the demand had Retention been deductible; and

   (iii) state the amount demanded, which shall not exceed the amount stated pursuant to clause 4(ii), and identify for which one or more of the following such amount is demanded:

   (a) the costs actually incurred by the Employer by reason of the failure of the Contractor to comply with the instructions of the Architect under the Contract; and be accompanied by a statement by the Architect which confirms that this failure by the Contractor has occurred;

   (b) the insurance premiums paid by the Employer pursuant to the Contract because the Contractor has not taken out and/or not maintained any insurance of the building works which he was required under the Contract to take out and/or maintain;

   (c) liquidated and ascertained damages which under the Contract the Contractor is due to pay or allow to the Employer; and be accompanied by a copy of the certificate of the Architect which under the Contract he is required to issue and which certifies that the Contractor has failed to complete the works by the contractual Completion Date;

   (d) any expenses or any direct loss and/or damage caused to the Employer as a result of the determination of the employment of the Contractor by the Employer;

   (e) any costs, other than the amounts referred to in clauses 4(iii)(a), (b), (c) and (d), which the Employer has actually incurred and which, under the Contract, he is entitled to deduct from monies otherwise due or to become due to the Contractor; and identify his entitlement;

   and

   (iv) incorporate a certification that the Contractor has been given 14 days' written notice of his liability for the amount demanded hereunder by the Employer and that the Contractor has not discharged that liability; and that a copy of this notice has at the same time been sent to the Surety at its office at

   _____

See Note 3

Such demand as above shall, for the purposes of this Bond but not further or otherwise, be conclusive evidence (and admissible as such) that the amount demanded is properly due and payable to the Employer by the Contractor.

5   If the Contract is to be assigned or otherwise transferred with the benefit of this Bond, the Employer shall be entitled to assign or transfer this Bond only with the prior written consent of the Surety, such consent not to be unreasonably delayed or withheld.

6   The Surety, in the absence of a prior written demand made, shall be released from its liability under this Bond upon the earliest occurrence of either

   (i)   the date of issue under the Contract of the Certificate of Completion of Making Good Defects; or

   (ii) satisfaction of a demand(s) up to the maximum aggregate under the Bond; or

See Note 4

   (iii) _____ (insert calendar date).

7 Any demand made hereunder must be received by the Surety accompanied by the documents as required by clause 4 above on or before the earliest occurrence as stated above, when this Bond will terminate and become of no further effect whatsoever.

8 Notwithstanding any other provisions of this Bond nothing in this Bond confers or purports to confer any right to enforce any of its terms on any person who is not a party to it.

9 This Bond shall be governed and construed in accordance with the laws of England and Wales.

IN WITNESS hereof this Bond has been executed as a Deed by the Surety and delivered on the date below:

EXECUTED as a Deed by: _____

for and on behalf of the Surety: _____

EXECUTED as a Deed by: _____

for and on behalf of the Employer: _____

Date: _____

Notes

These Notes will not appear on the Bond issued by the Surety.

1 The terms of Annex 3 have been discussed with the British Bankers' Association and the Surety Panel of the Association of British Insurers. The Tribunal understands that a Bond which embodies the terms of this Annex is, at the proposed Surety's discretion, available to Contractors where the Employer has incorporated into the building contract on the Standard Form of Building Contract 1998 Edition, Private version, incorporating Amendments 1 to _____, the optional clause 30·4A.

2 The figure to be inserted here is the amount stated in the Appendix pursuant to clause 30·4A·2. It is understood that a Surety will, at additional cost to the Contractor, and which may be subject to other terms and conditions of the Surety, provide for a greater sum than that stated in clause 2 if, due to variations, and had Retention been applicable, that amount would have increased. The reduction by 50% of the maximum aggregate sum at the date of issue of the next Interim Certificate after Practical Completion matches a similar reduction had Retention been applicable.

3 The inclusion in clause 4 of the words "but not further or otherwise" is to make clear that the Contractor would not be prevented by the terms of clause 4 from alleging, under the Contract, that the Contractor was not in breach on any of the matters stated in clause 4(iii)(a) to (e).

Any demand by the Employer under clause 4 of this Bond must not exceed the costs actually incurred by the Employer and is not to be in excess of the amount stated in clause 4(ii).

4 The Surety requires an actual expiry date or (if earlier) a date that is capable of being ascertained on the face of the Bond. Where this is not possible, alternative terms should be discussed with the Surety.

Private With Quantities

This reprint incorporates the following amendments.

A **Amendment 1, June 1999**
Construction Industry Scheme (CIS)
(incorporated September 2000)

1. **Recitals**
   Fourth recital amended
2. **Clause 30**
   new clause 30·4 A inserted
3. **Clause 31**
   redrafted
4. **Appendix**
   entry on Fourth recital amended

B **Amendment 2, January 2000**
Sundry amendments
(incorporated September 2000)

1. **Clause 1·12**
   new clause inserted
2. **Clause 30**
   clause 30·1·3 amended
3. **Clause 41A**
   clause 41A·5·5·2 amended
   new clause 41A·5·8 inserted
   new footnote [uu·1] inserted
4. **Appendix**
   entry on 30·1·3 amended
   new footnote [aaa·1] inserted
   entry on 41A·2 amended

   Fluctuation clauses
   (published separately)
   clauses 38·2·1 and ·2 amended
   clause 38·2·3 deleted
   clause 38·6·2 amended
   clauses 39·3·1, ·2 and ·3 amended
   clause 39·3·4 deleted
   clause 39·7·2 amended

C **Additions and corrections made and incorporated in reprint dated September 2000**

1. **Clause 30·4A**
   optional clause and Annex 3 incorporated
2. **"pay"/"paid" substituted for "discharge(d)"**
   clauses 27·6·2·2 and 27·6·4·1
   clause 30·6·2·1
   clauses 35·13·5·2 and 35·13·5·3·3
3. **Minor corrections to wording, upper and lower case, punctuation etc.**
   throughout contract

D **Amendment 3, January 2001**
Terrorism cover, Joint Fire Code, CIS, SMM
(incorporated May 2001)

1. **Clause 1·3**
   definition amended for 'Joint Fire Code'
   definition inserted for 'Standard Method of Measurement'
   footnote [n] deleted
   references to footnote [n] deleted in definitions for 'Approximate Quantity' and 'provisional sum' and in clauses 2·2·2·2, 13·5·3·3, 13·5·5, 25·4·5·1 and 26·2·7
2. **Clause 2·2**
   clauses 2·2·2·1 and 2·2·2·2 amended
3. **Clause 13·5**
   clauses 13·5·3·3 and 13·5·6·4 amended
4. **Clause 22·2**
   amended, and definitions inserted for 'terrorism' and 'terrorism cover'
5. **Clause 22A**
   new clause 22A·5 inserted
6. **Clause 22B**
   new clause 22B·4 inserted
7. **Clause 22C**
   new clauses 22C·1A and 22C·5 inserted
8. **Clause 22FC**
   clause 22FC·3 amended
   clause 22FC·4 deleted
   clause 22FC·5 amended
9. **Clause 30·4A**
   clause 30·4A·1 amended
10. **Clause 31**
    clauses 31·10 and 31·11 amended
    footnote [oo·2] inserted
11. **Clause 35**
    clause 35·1 amended
12. **Appendix**
    new entry on 22FC·5 inserted

E **Correction made and incorporated in reprint dated May 2001**

VAT Agreement
clause 5: minor correction

F **Amendment 4, January 2002**
Extension of time/Loss and expense/Advance payment
(incorporated October 2002)

1. **Clause 25**
   new clause 25·4·19 inserted
2. **Clause 26**
   new clause 26·2·11 inserted
3. **Clause 30**
   clause 30·2 amended

G **Corrections**
(incorporated October 2002)

1. **Clauses 8·1·4, 22D·1, 42·15**
   'delayed or withheld' substituted for 'withheld or delayed'
2. **Minor corrections to wording, punctuation, etc**
   throughout contract
3. **Annexes 1 and 3**
   Minor amendments, some required by BBA
4. **Statutory references**
   VAT and SERPS references updated

H **Amendment 5, July 2003**
Construction Skills Certification Scheme
(incorporated September 2003)

1. **Clause 8**
   clause 8·1·4 renumbered as clause 8·1·5
   new clause 8·1·4 inserted